Will You Run Out of Money Before You Run Out of Life?

PLANNING & STRATEGY
FOR A SOUND FINANCIAL FUTURE

Michael Niemczyk

Michael Niemczyk
10 North Lake Street
Grayslake, IL 60030
www.mlnrp.com

Book layout ©2013 BookDesignTemplates.com

Michael Niemczyk/Will You Run Out of Money Before You Run Out of Life? —1st ed.
ISBN 9781075266294

This book is designed to provide you with information about your finances and preparing for retirement. It is not designed to be, and should not be construed as, investment advice or a recommendation of any kind.

We are a financial services firm helping clients plan for retirement through the use of insurance and investment products. Investment advisory services offered through MLN Retirement Planning, Inc., a Registered Investment Advisor. We do not offer tax or legal advice. Always consult with your own qualified tax/legal advisors concerning your unique situation.

Investing involves risk, including possible loss of principal. No investment strategy ensures a profit or guarantees against a loss. Insurance product guarantees are backed by the financial strength and claims-paying ability of the issuing company.

Contents

By consultation, plans will succeed
And by skillful direction, wage your war

—PROVERBS 20:18 *(NWT)*

To my beautiful wife, Leah, who always has my back. Thank you for being such a loving mother to our children. You complete me and give me the security to accomplish more. I couldn't imagine life any other way.

To Mikey and Ella. If it wasn't for you, I would have had this book completed earlier! But you are the reason I get up and work hard. I love you. You inspire me to do my best so you can one day say, "I have the best dad."

To my MLN team members, who are there for me and our company day in and day out. You're on the front lines, allowing for the words in this book to come to fruition. You smile and say yes when it may not come easy. You, I consider family.

To my mother, Theresa, who instilled in me a strong work ethic and the drive to "just keep going." You always display unconditional love and are always smiling—thank you for passing that on to us.

To my wonderful sisters, Kristy and Nikki, who are there through good times and difficult ones. From the days of us playing "jobs," you helped mold me into a better person. Kristy, you make MLN possible.

To GG, if it wasn't for you, I wouldn't have taken up writing in the first place. You always corrected us on our speech when we were younger and have been inspirational to me. Thank you for being my "go-to for life."

To Uncle Vinny, who has helped me stay on the right path. You have always been reliable and available even when inconvenient, encouraging me to grow in every area of my life. Thanks for setting such a fine example.

Introduction

Before you crack this book open, please understand who this book is written for. It's for those planning for retirement or those in retirement. Although it's not partial to age, it *isn't* a double-your-money-in-two-years or a get-rich-quick, silver-bullet-secret strategy. Discussions in this book may go against mainstream advisory practices. Yet, these are time-tested, reliable strategies to help you navigate through the complex world of retirement planning. So, enjoy!

- "How much money will we need to retire?"
- "Can I leave anything for my children? If so, how much?"
- "How will we afford health care?"
- "Should we pay off the house and car before we retire? Buy a second home now by dipping into our retirement funds?"

If you are near or at retirement, have you asked similar questions? You're not alone. These are just a few of the questions our firm gets from individuals when we're discussing their options and needs for retirement. But the one I hear most often is this: "Will I run out of money before I run out of life?"

This is something new. Our parents' and grandparents' main concern was not living long *enough* to enjoy retirement. Just look at Social Security as an example. When it was started in 1935 the average life expectancy was sixty-two; just at the time a person should be receiving their benefit, they were dead. Running out of money before running out of life is a serious question that deserves a thoughtful, thorough answer.

The good news is we're living longer and healthier lives. Thanks to medical science and smarter lifestyle choices, there were more than 72,000 people alive in 2014 who were a hundred years old or beyond, according to a report from the Centers for Disease Control and Prevention. By 2055, that number could approach 500,000.[1]

The bad news is your money for retirement will most likely have to last you longer than anyone could have realistically projected even twenty years ago. The idea of budgeting and living off your investments to age eighty was pretty intimidating to begin with. Now add ten or twenty more years to that and you can see why people are concerned. Social Security and Medicare (Medicare being the government health care program for those with disabilities or those sixty-five and over)—currently underfunded and encumbered with more than $50 trillion in combined unfunded liability—and just about every other government program should be evaluated for their long-term solvency.[2]

What about you? What channels of income are you relying on? Are you relying on a pension? The pensions our parents and grandparents depended on have all but disappeared from the private sector. Some of those that remain are underfunded. A large shift from defined-benefit pensions to defined-contribution plans—your 401(k)—has taken place. Millions of retirees are being forced into becoming their own financial advisors. Add to that an

---

[1] Marissa Fessenden. Smithsonian.com. January 22, 2016. "There Are Now More Americans Over Age 100 and They're Living Longer Than Ever." https://www.smithsonianmag.com/smart-news/there-are-more-americans-over-age-100-now-and-they-are-living-longer-180957914/.

[2] James C. Capretta. MarketWatch. June 16, 2018. "Opinion: The financial hole for Social Security and Medicare is even deeper than the experts say." https://www.marketwatch.com/story/the-financial-hole-for-social-security-and-medicare-is-even-deeper-than-the-experts-say-2018-06-15

environment of low interest rates and continuous stock market volatility, and it's clear why planning for retirement these days is a challenge.

Surveys tell us that more than half—about 67 percent—of retired investors in this country are concerned they may outlive their savings. Many people simply haven't saved enough.

Some lost a lot of money during the Tech Bubble of 2000 to 2001 or the Great Recession of 2008 to 2009.[3] Some are still hesitant to put money in the stock market even though it offers the greatest growth potential.

I believe many Americans are not properly educated about finances, and at the same time there are also many financial professionals who are insufficiently trained to help them prepare for retirement today. If I can contribute toward offering solutions, even if it's one person at a time, I feel it is worthwhile.

My desire to help people with their retirement planning started when I was still in college. My mother and father were blue-collar workers, doing their jobs and putting away savings so they could enjoy their later years without wondering, "Are we going to run out of money?" One day nearly twenty-five years ago, I vividly remember my father on the landline phone, ten-foot cord and all, in the kitchen with their investment "guru" telling them they'd lost a substantial amount of their savings. Almost from that minute, I decided to learn as much as I could about finances and investments and how to protect other people from this experience. I started my own firm after working for a large investment and insurance company. I wasn't happy with being a "captive" advisor. Being "captive" meant I could only design plans around and offer whatever strategies and products the company I worked for. It seemed very

---

[3] Emmie Martin. CNBC. May 14, 2018. "67% of Americans say they'll outlive their retirement savings."

https://www.cnbc.com/2018/05/11/how-many-americans-have-no-retirement-savings.html.

"fixed," and I wondered at how that could be in the best interest of the client or investor. So, in 2001, I opened Michael Niemczyk & Associates, Inc., which morphed into MLN Retirement Planning, Inc., in my hometown, with the goal of helping people aged fifty and older, or those ten years or less out from retirement. From just me and one desk, it's grown to a team with a dozen members, helping more than several hundred individuals, families, and corporations. I can confidently look our clients in the eye and know I am helping them build the right plan to make sure they will not face the same situation as my parents.

I want to ask you the same question I ask those clients: What do you feel is the financial basis for a successful retirement? In my professional experience, what matters most is not solely the size of your assets like your 401(k), IRA, bank account, home, and other possessions. It's what you do with them. Assets can be lost or seriously depleted in a variety of ways. They can be wiped out through divorce, fraud, a lawsuit, market crash, taxes, or paying for long-term health care. Assets are just numbers on a piece of paper. The biggest question you need to ask yourself as a retiree is this: How do I create an income from my assets that continues for as long as I need, regardless of stock market, economic, and governmental uncertainty?

It is just another way of asking the question on the cover of this book: Will I run out of money before I run out of life?

This book is here to help you find an answer to that question and to offer some time-tested strategies for you to consider if the answer isn't looking good. A good investment strategy helps address three things: It protects your principal, gives you a reliable income for life, and helps keep up with inflation. You may have principal protection and income for life. But many ignore that third aspect. The principal that you're drawing income from needs to keep up with higher payments and costs in the future. I believe this is a key ingredient.

To help make that happen, many of my suggestions will focus on three areas: income planning, tax planning, and asset protection. I'll discuss some of the mistakes I've seen people make (including myself) and how to avoid them in your own retirement planning. Nobody loves to spend their free time reading about dense financial matters. I appreciate that and hope to make this a learning experience that is enjoyable and easy to understand. My goal is for you to complete this book and be more knowledgeable, better prepared to act, and less concerned about running out of money before you run out of life.

CHAPTER 1

It's Never Too Late to Plan . . . Until It Is

Lily was a little apprehensive about consulting with an advisor. In her late fifties at the time, she'd been let go from her company earlier than she had planned and hoped for. Her main assets were two pharmaceutical stocks worth a little over half a million dollars that her parents had left her years ago! Although she was unaware of the actual value, she was living off the dividends of those—about $1,500 a month. She had considerable personal debt and went without medical treatments because her insurance was inadequate. The dividends from her stock were not enough to cover normal living expenses for Lily, who was trying to follow her parents' example.

Lily's parents had been very conservative, financially. They had pensions and lived very frugally. Therefore, they had only taken the dividends themselves, so for several years Lily did the same thing. This is a common thread among investors. They do what they see or have been taught, although their beliefs and circumstances are completely different. For instance, if your parents are Catholic, chances are you're Catholic. Lily's stocks were in well-known companies that were unlikely to go bankrupt, but she was still overexposed to market fluctuations, and the income from them was negligible. She was also paying out about $2,700 a month in credit card and other debt services. That may not sound like a lot, but it's a Goliath when your income is so small.

Lily was also extremely risk averse. She didn't want to take on any risk of losing even a small portion of her life savings, which was one reason she was so apprehensive about seeking help. She thought meeting with a retirement planner or investment advisor might expose her to even *more* loss. However, because she didn't understand the statements that were coming in regarding her pharmaceutical stocks, she had no idea of the risk she was already experiencing. She needed help.

In a situation like Lily's, we would want to look at ways to establish an income source or to get interest payments without subjecting what's left of a nest egg to the whims of the market. But perhaps most importantly, we'd want to look at how to dial down or eliminate that debt. That alone would free up thousands of dollars in income per month.

Lily's story highlights several of the most common mistakes people make with their assets as they reach or near retirement:

- Too conservative/not understanding risk
- Emotional connection to holdings
- Trust issues with financial professionals

Many people are so conservative with their money that the money they *do* have isn't able to work for them. Effectively, Lily had stuffed hers into the mattress, forcing her to reduce her standard of living substantially. Paradoxically, she was also taking a big risk by having her entire nest egg in the stock market, even though it was invested in well-known stocks perceived as "safe." You can't justify saying, "Okay, we're going be safe and just take those 3 percent dividends" when your entire portfolio is in the market and thus at risk. That's not a fair trade-off, in my opinion. By not using her assets to establish a reliable income, she was depleting her principal (through monthly credit card and other debt service payments) when she didn't need to. Unfortunately, what often happens in that situation is that people take on even more risk because of the panic that starts to set in because of shrinking retirement assets. And that compounds the problem.

In the preceding story, Lily's behavior was driven by another trait common to investors: She had an emotional connection to the portfolio. To Lily, those stocks were sacred because they'd belonged to her parents. Her father had worked for the pharmaceutical company. He hadn't made much of a salary but had accumulated these stocks. That made changing her investments more difficult, emotionally speaking.

Many investors inadvertently downsize their retirement income and thereby downsize their dreams. We see folks who have considerably more than Lily's assets, but they look at them as untouchable, without realizing what their assets can really bring them in terms of income.

Here's the third common mistake: Some people are uneasy about putting their financial affairs into a professional's hands. Some have legitimate trust issues based on bad past experiences. But while it's appropriate to use those experiences to inform your future decisions, it's a bad idea to let them inhibit you or prevent you from following good advice. No matter who is referring you to an advisor, the choice is ultimately your own.

One positive lesson we can learn from Lily's story is, even later in life, you can still take the reins and get in control of things—as long as you haven't let them go too far, as the next story illustrates.

Some time back, I met with a prospective client, who we'll call Frank, was retiring after years of working for a major cosmetics company. He had over a million dollars in his retirement plan, mostly invested in mutual funds and other stocks he'd built up through his 401(k). His goal was to live off the interest.

Frank and his wife had two homes, one in Illinois and one on a lake in Wisconsin. They lived a pretty free-spending lifestyle to boot. When the Great Recession hit and the market dropped in 2008 to 2009, they lost half of their life savings but they continued spending the same amount and living as they had grown accustomed to. That doesn't work. If you have a million dollars and you're pulling off $70,000 or $80,000, that's one thing. But if you're at $500,000 and you're still pulling off $80,000, you're toast. The poor guy came to me because he didn't have the guts to tell his wife. He knew it was bad. "We're in trouble," Frank told me.

He knew they were going to have to sell one of their homes and lose much of what he'd worked so hard for—all because his financial advisor led him to believe this portfolio was the answer to having a successful retirement. All along, Frank was never provided with any solid evidence to back up those claims. By the time he realized the problem, it was too late. Truthfully, he and the advisor had never discussed how his portfolio worked in connection with his lifestyle of overspending. Frank walked into a flashy glass high-rise, looked around the office and figured, "Wow, these guys must know what they're doing." The advisor talked him into high risk/high reward investments with a set-it-and-forget-it outlook, and ultimately allowed his clients' nest egg to be devastated.

Although Frank's circumstances were dire, he still had a lot of faith in the advisor. So, what did he want from me? He wanted someone to not only bail out the advisor and the problem he created, but he also wanted to "pull the rabbit out of the hat," finding a solution that didn't involve some consequences. He needed my help to figure out how to manage all this with what was left.

At that point, I had to tell him there was little I could do other than to put them on an extremely tight budget if he was unwilling to change his expectations. Unfortunately, Frank came to me too late. Not that we couldn't have helped him. We could have! We are experienced in putting together plans that would have put him on track for recovery, and after some years of cutting back he would have had the chance to enjoy some of what he had before. The fact that he and his wife were trying to live the lifestyle they had dreamed of—something all retirees deserve—wasn't the issue. The fault lies first and foremost with the advisor and the advisor's plan. But the investor must also take some responsibility for not getting a second opinion and asking for evidence that his portfolio could sustain itself in times of trouble (in this case, the Great Recession).

There are a few morals here. One is never to allow too much time to pass before seeking a second opinion and another is about being sure your plan can adapt when times change. Frank gambled and lost because of his unfounded faith in his advisor, and because he waited too long before consulting another financial professional. But the underlying reason for all this failure has to do with taking on too much market risk. We will address this and much more in the next chapter.

CHAPTER 2

Ten Major Risks to Your Retirement

Many people face one or more major risks to their financial well-being during retirement. All people will likely face at least some of them. Which are you most concerned about? We will return to some of these in more detail throughout the book and talk about ways to avoid each of them.

1. Stock market
2. Sequence of return
3. Loss of spouse
4. Health
5. Withdrawals/distributions
6. Inflation
7. Tax
8. Forced retirement
9. Bailing out kids
10. Longevity

Stock Market

Like death and taxes, stock market risk can feel virtually inescapable. In my experience, perhaps the No. 1 mistake retirees fail to recognize is investing *for* retirement is different from investing *during* retirement. When we are in our working years, we're in an accumulating stage, adding money to our investments month over month, growing our nest egg. During this period of saving, you may not pay much attention to stock market fluctuations, reasoning that time is on your side. In retirement though, we are in a spending, or distribution, stage. Because of this, there needs to be a shift in the level of risk you're willing to accept or can allow.

When it comes to your portfolio, what is risk tolerance? Bottom line: It means asking how much you are willing to lose! If you were to ask your neighbor, advisor, and co-worker to define a moderate portfolio, you could get three different answers. Would you agree with this statement?

The truth is, you are in charge of your own "risk tolerance;" no one else is responsible for it or can determine it for you. Therefore, the issue is investors load up on risk, either knowingly or unknowingly, and their perception of risk can differ from the reality. Of course, no one loves losing money to the market. But in a market downturn, some may reason it will only take five to ten years to recover and so they just keep on investing. Others, particularly retirees, don't have that option—they need the income to cover today's bills and can't wait five to ten years to get that money back.

Sequence of Returns

Listen up! Sequence of returns risk refers to the impact of market gains and losses on a portfolio during the years you are living wholly or partially off it. The risk comes in the form of low or negative returns, which have a multiplying effect on the withdrawals taken by the retiree for everyday living expenses. That accelerates a portfolio's rate of depletion. If hit hard enough at the outset, a retiree will have a difficult time recovering, which increases the likelihood that he or she will run out of money long before running out of life.

Consider that in the Great Recession, the average stock fund lost nearly 40 percent.[4] For investors in the fifty-plus age bracket, a demographic quickly closing in on retirement, the loss had a greater impact than on those in younger brackets. Think about losing more than a third of your net worth at a time when you need those funds for expenses such as gas, utilities, groceries, and health care.

The following illustration will demonstrate how sequence-of-return risk works.

Let me set the stage. John and Mary—a hypothetical couple—have both decided to retire. They both need an income of $25,000 a year to start with, plus a cost-of-living adjustment to combat inflation. As you will see in the chart, Mary retired at the beginning of a sustained market rise while John did so at the beginning of a decline. Both needed about the same amount of income from their investments to live on, but withdrawing that money carried significantly different consequences for each. John lost 10.1 percent the first year, 13 percent the second and 23.4 percent the third. Is this scenario realistic? Can this actually happen? Of course it can! Poor John worked forty years to finally experience the fruits of his labor. However, the market doesn't care. That's why it's so important to get your portfolio off on the right foot. John's loss of 46.5 percent during those years is compounded by his withdrawal of $77,273 for living expenses.

---

[4] Katy Marquardt. U.S. News & World Report. January 7, 2009. "If Your Stock Fund Lost Less Than 38% in 2008, You're Lucky."

https://money.usnews.com/money/blogs/new-money/2009/01/07/if-your-stock-fund-lost-less-than-38-in-2008-youre-gold.

JOHN

AGE	Gains	Withdrawal	Savings
64			$500,000
65	-10.14%	$25,000.00	$500,000
66	-13.04%	$25,750.00	$426,835.00
67	-23.37%	$26,522.50	$348,783.52
68	14.62%	$27,318.18	$246,948.62
69	2.03%	$28,137.72	$251,740.41
70	12.40%	$28,981.85	$228,141.83
71	27.25%	$29,851.31	$223,855.81
72	-6.65%	$30,746.85	$246,870.73
73	26.31%	$31,669.25	$201,751.65
74	4.46%	$32,619.33	$214,831.07
75	7.06%	$33,597.91	$190,338.39
76	-1.54%	$34,605.85	$167,806.35
77	34.11%	$35,644.02	$131,149.22
78	20.26%	$36,713.34	$128,082.02
79	31.01%	$37,814.74	$109,879.97
80	26.67%	$38,949.19	$94,412.66
81	19.53%	$40,117.66	$70,255.58
82	26.38%	$36,023.85	$36,023.85
83	-38.49%	$0.00	$0.00
84	3.00%		
85	13.62%		
86	3.53%		
87	26.38%		
88	23.45%		
89	12.78%		

This example is shown for illustrative purposes only and does not reflect investment fees or taxes, which would reduce the figures shown here.

MARY

AGE	Gains	Withdrawal	Savings
64			$500,000
65	12.78%	$25,000.00	$500,000
66	23.45%	$25,750.00	$535,705.00
67	26.38%	$26,522.50	$629,539.45
68	3.53%	$27,318.18	$762,092.82
69	13.62%	$28,137.72	$760,712.19
70	3.00%	$28,981.85	$832,351.11
71	-38.49%	$29,851.31	$827,470.34
72	26.38%	$30,746.85	$490,615.46
73	19.53%	$31,669.25	$581,181.96
74	26.67%	$32,619.33	$656,832.54
75	31.01%	$33,597.91	$790,690.87
76	20.26%	$34,605.85	$991,867.49
77	34.11%	$35,644.02	$1,151,202.85
78	-1.54%	$36,713.34	$1,496,075.95
79	7.06%	$37,814.74	$1,436,888.42
80	4.46%	$38,949.19	$1,497,848.28
81	26.31%	$40,117.66	$1,523,965.99
82	-6.65%	$41,321.19	$1,874,248.83
83	27.25%	$42,560.83	$1,711,037.95
84	12.40%	$43,837.65	$2,123,137.14
85	2.03%	$45,152.78	$2,337,132.63
86	14.62%	$46,507.36	$2,338,507.04
87	-23.37%	$47,902.59	$2,627,090.02
88	-13.04%	$49,339.66	$1,976,431.33
89	-10.14%	$50,819.85	$1,731,684.58

This example is shown for illustrative purposes only and does not reflect investment fees or taxes, which would reduce the figures shown here.

As we can see, John runs out of money at age eighty-three. Mary also worked forty years to finally enjoy her nest egg and life-style she planned for. It may appear that Mary timed her retirement perfectly. Actually, she experienced the same percentage of losses as John. However, it wasn't until several years into retirement, which gave her portfolio a chance to grow. She amasses $1.7 million by age eighty-nine. The takeaway from this example is twofold. Firstly, making sure your life's work is protected from losses, especially early on, is of the utmost importance. The second is that the average rate of return isn't the same as actual rate of return. The average rate of return for both investors is the same— 8.03 percent—but the real rate of return is much different. John's situation isn't a pleasant scenario. Unfortunately, magazines, advertisements, and broker illustrations market their returns using average, not actual, rates of return. That can have significant effects on someone solely relying on the final rate of return. It can be deceiving and highlights the importance of receiving complete and accurate information when evaluating a retirement portfolio. In any event, concrete steps must be taken to help minimize unnecessary risk and ensure that investors don't outlive their assets.

Loss of Spouse

Many couples rely on one spouse's pension or Social Security benefits. Statistics show it's common for one spouse to outlive the other one, often by many years. Typically, the husband dies before his wife. No, not because he wants to, it's just statistically true of men. When that spouse is no longer around, the surviving spouse could face a significant decrease in monthly income. Have you and your spouse talked about this possibility and worked on a way of filling the void in respect to your income plan?

Some couples don't take the time to discuss these matters. But, difficult as it is, they need to be addressed. Don't wait until it's too late. Failing to plan for this likely event can cause major problems for the surviving spouse when the deceased's pension or Social Security benefits are heavily relied upon.

The Financial Consequences of Losing a Spouse

When it comes to losing a spouse, it goes without saying what gut-wrenching emotional trauma one has to deal with. When you couple the emotional loss with the financial loss, individuals can be so overwhelmed it's as if they're paralyzed. Planning ahead of time with strategies to combat the financial loss is paramount, no matter how uncomfortable.

Take for example a married couple, Bob and Jane, who are both receiving Social Security and other income totaling $100,000 annually. Let's say each of them receives $2,000 in taxable income from Social Security each month. Using the current standard deduction of $24,000 for filing jointly, Bob and Jane's taxable income becomes $76,000. With current tax rates, they would owe approximately $8,732 in federal taxes in a given year.

Bob & Jane Taxes 2018 Married Filing Jointly

$100,000	Gross Income
-$24,000	Standard Deduction
$76,000	Taxable Income
$8,732	Taxes
$91,268	Net Income After Federal Tax

Bob passes away suddenly. Just as sudden, Jane loses Bob's $2,000 monthly check from Social Security. Jane's annual income now drops to $76,000. She has to decide what $2,000 part of her monthly budget she's going to get rid of. Is it going to be travel? Will she have to give up spending on experiences with the grand-kids? Might she have to cut back on her daily necessities? Is it going to be difficult to pay property taxes? All of these perils and tough decisions rear their ugly heads. But unknown to Jane, she is also bearing additional tax consequences.

Not only does Jane now have a significant reduction of income, she now also loses half her standard deduction, which drops from $24,000 to $12,200 because she's now filing single. And filing single means she's in a higher tax bracket, according to current rates. In this case, Jane now ends up owing $9,895 in federal taxes. When all is said and done, Jane 1) lost Bob's Social Security, 2) has only $12,200 as a standard deduction, and 3) pays $1,163 more in taxes!

Jane Taxes in 2019 Filing Single (Widowed)

$76,000	Gross Income
-$12,200	Standard Deduction
$63,800	Taxable Income
$9,895	Taxes
$66,105	Net Income After Federal Tax

Spousal Income Lost: $24,000
Actual NET Income Lost: $25,163

If you're married, what is your plan to combat this increase in taxes and loss of income? What has your advisor done to protect you from this potential loss? Whoever you're paying to manage your assets, have they brought this conversation up with you?

Health and Long-Term Care Expenses

Medical costs and long-term care expenses are like monsters stalking your retirement plan, potentially eating up your nest egg at a dizzying pace. Sound dramatic? A recent study revealed that a typical sixty-five-year-old couple will need approximately $280,000 to pay for unreimbursed medical expenses throughout their retirement years. This does not include long-term care, which seven out of ten sixty-five-year-olds will need some form of during their lifetime. So, as a retiree, how do you plan on handling this issue?[5]

You have several options:

1) You may choose to have a separate or allocated amount of funds to cover these needs.

2) You may choose to "roll the dice" so to speak. You may reason that your family history is invincible and you don't get sick, so you decide to not pay it any attention.

3) You decide to use leverage via long-term care (LTC) insurance coverage.

Regarding long-term care, you may acknowledge, "Yes, this is a serious concern for me (or us)." But naturally there are so many questions regarding LTC coverage. For starters, traditional long-term care insurance can be expensive! "What if we are not in the statistical majority? What if we never need the long-term care? What happens to all the money we have paid for something we've never used? Poof, gone!?" Another concern is LTC can be difficult to qualify for. "I'm not a twenty-five-year-old marathon runner. I (like most retirees) have gone through some tough times so no, I'm sorry I'm not in perfect health." Lastly, say you have decided to acquire LTC insurance, and at first the coverage and financial obligation fit your budget. However, as you age, what if the premiums get more expensive?

All these issues are real. So, is there a prudent way to address the need for long-term care solutions without breaking the bank? The insurance industry has actually made major changes to help answer this question. Like going from VHS to Netflix streaming,

---

[5] Fidelity. April 19, 2018. "A Couple Retiring in 2018 Would Need an Estimated $280,000 to Cover Health Care Costs in Retirement, Fidelity Analysis Shows."

https://www.fidelity.com/about-fidelity/employer-services/a-couple-retiring-in-2018-would-need-estimated-280000.

there are now solutions. The combo life insurance/chronic illness care policy. Besides being a mouthful, what is that? This is a way to get a level of protection within a life insurance policy, offering two benefits in one product. But even better is that this is not a use-it-or-lose-it situation.

So let's play out a few scenarios with this product:

1) You pass away and never used the long-term care rider of your policy. The remaining death benefit goes to your family or whomever you name—tax free!

2) Let's say you need care, then you would begin to peel off a monthly amount to cover your long-term care need. It simply reduces the death benefit, or the amount that goes to your beneficiaries when you die. But you're using the money, so it is not lost.

3) If you aren't in need of long-term care but down the road you decide you want to take a loan or withdrawal from the accumulated cash value within your policy, you can do so tax free! You will pay an interest rate to receive that money, and the policy cash values and death benefit will be reduced by the amount of any withdrawals but, unless your policy has become a modified endowment contract, your withdrawals won't be taxed.

In short, medical costs and long-term care expenses do not need to be the monsters that they are for so many people.

Forced Retirement

Your retirement may come sooner than you planned, and not by choice. You may have thirty, forty, or even more years on the job. You see yourself five years away from retirement, anticipating that everything will be smooth sailing and you'll glide perfectly into the bay of retirement, like James Bond in "Man with the Golden Gun."

But your employer may have other plans. Unfortunately, they might see you as an over-paid, over-qualified, expensive liability to the company. Or perhaps the company is restructuring. Or it's having a hard time financially and lays you off. Since you believed you were five years away from retirement, you've kept more risk in your portfolio than you would have otherwise. How do you prepare for this realistic change of circumstances?

Bailing Out Kids

Picture this: You have raised wonderful children. You are such a good parent. How do I know? Because Junior is still at home, over forty, still asking mom to make him a PB&J. You have no issue with it. Admittedly, I can see myself doing the same thing, though I can't attest to my own children being in similar circumstances, since they are currently ages fourteen and two. The risk we're talking about here is that your ability to pay for this personal matter could be compromised. I have clients who continue to work and forgo retirement for more than a decade because their kids choose not to work! Or, worse yet, maybe the child moves their spouse and three kids into the house while none of them are working, counting on your work to support them.

Supporting children to this degree is a prerogative for many parents. Without saying whether that's right or wrong, it does need to be addressed in your plan. It's one thing to prepare for your own financial emergencies and lifestyle. What I see all too often are loving parents, close to or in retirement, unexpectedly trying to help out adult children financially. Surveys show more than six out of ten people over the age of fifty have given financial support to a family member within the past five years. The bottom line is that if you're as generous as described, you need to account for this often-unpredictable risk.[6]

---

[6] Pew Research Center. May 21, 2015. "Family Support in Greying Societies." http://www.pewsocialtrends.org/2015/05/21/family-support-in-graying-societies/.

Withdrawal Rate

One common understanding you may read in magazines or hear from advisors is that you can be confident that an average rate of return will cover an income withdrawal of about 3 to 4 percent. What if you need more, say twice that amount? How will that impact your portfolio and ability to make your funds last? This is a problem on its own. But now we need to couple that with a down market, recession, or even depression. A retiree likely will not have the time or the principal to recover. Think this can't happen to you? Let's talk history. Here are the market downturns, the "bear markets" of the past ninety years:[7]

1. September 1929 – June 1932
    -86.1% in 34 months
2. May 1946 – June 1949
    -29.6% in 37 months
3. December 1961 – June 1962
    -28.0% in 6 months
4. November 1968 – May 1970
    -36.1% in 18 months
5. January 1973 – October 1974
    -48.0% in 21 months
6. November 1980 – August 1982
    -27.8% in 21 months
7. August 1987 – December 1987
    -33.5% in 4 months

---

[7] First Trust Portfolios. Dec. 31, 2018. "History of U.S. Bear and Bull Markets." https://www.ftportfolios.com/Common/ContentFileLoader.aspx?Content-GUID=4ecfa978-d0bb-4924-92c8-628ff9bfe12d.

8. March 2000 – October 2002
   -49.1% in 30 months
9. October 2007 – March 2009
   -56.4% in 17 months

The average life expectancy is eighty-five to ninety years. Now tell me the market can't impact your retirement. There's no need to imagine it; it has happened to others. It is quite possible according to statistics, in your lifetime nine "bears" could "eat" into your savings. So, back to the point: When the whole of your savings is needed to produce that regular withdrawal rate for income but at the same time you are open to market downturns, this makes for a detrimental, if not impossible, reliance upon your portfolio.

Inflation Risk

Inflation is sometimes referred to as a "silent threat" to retirement plans. Why? Inflation has a compounding effect. Each and every year, whether you notice or not, it can eat away at your spending power. Regardless of the rate of inflation claimed by the government, you feel the true rate if you've paid for health insurance, a child's college, or simply a bag of groceries. Inflation can slowly creep up on us, year after year, decade after decade in a compounding fashion that many retirees never plan for. We could liken it to a frog thrown into a pot of water. If the water is boiling, the frog will jump right out. But what if the water is slowly brought up to boiling temperature? The frog will remain unaware of the increasing temperature until it's cooked. Don't be the frog; it's imperative you account for this in your income plan.

Inflation vs. Cost of Living

	1970	1985	Today	In 15 Years
Postage	$0.06	$0.22	$0.50	$0.80
College	$1,205	$3,372	$34,740	$46,165
Cars	$3,430	$11,925	$34,342	$56,542

The preceding chart's information comes from OfficialData.org's collection of the Consumer Price Index's inflation categories.[8]

Tax Risk

You can liken tax risk in retirement to playing the second half of a football game. Since I'm from the Chicago area, let's suppose da' Bears are playing the Green Bay Packers. I especially love using this illustration in Wisconsin. The Bears are beating the Packers 40-0 at halftime and had a record-breaking half on offense. Who is winning the game? The Bears, of course. But who has won the game? Unfortunately for the Bears, the game isn't over. We have two more quarters! As happens all too often, my Bears could still lose the lead and the game.

In retirement, wouldn't you agree you may have had a winning first half, your working years? You've saved very well, often earning double-digit growth on your money. And you've kept Uncle Sam from that money by using an IRA, 401(k), or similar plan. Now comes the second half, taking money out. You're no longer contributing but spending down, and thereby earning less. Isn't it possible that through your retirement years you could have been caught up in the return on your investment, failing to pay attention to what it will cost to withdraw the needed monthly income? When you withdraw and even when you pass away, these funds

---

[8] OfficialData.org. 2019. "Inflation Rates by CPI Category." https://www.officialdata.org/inflation-cpi-categories.

could be reduced significantly by taxes without a good defense. As this country gets further and further in debt and the so-called entitlements—Social Security and Medicare—become more and more underfunded, this poses a serious risk to your personal taxes and the likelihood of having them raised.

In retirement, typically there will be what I call the "three buckets" of money that generate income. Bucket 1 is taxable money. That is money you received from a paycheck or investment or business. Whether you spend it or not, whether you've (re)invested and it grows or you put it under your mattress, you have to pay income tax on it. Buying or selling within a non-qualified plan triggers capital gains and/or income tax. Obviously, a qualified plan offers an advantage with respect to accumulation.

Bucket 2 is tax-deferred money, such as in a 401(k), 403(b) retirement plan, traditional IRA, annuity, etc. In this bucket you do not pay taxes on the money as it accumulates.

However, the caveat to Bucket 2 is, when you take the money out of these accounts, you will pay taxes on them at your current income tax bracket, and may pay an additional 10 percent federal penalty if you are under age fifty-nine-and-one-half. We call this "delayed taxation."

Bucket 3 is tax-exempt, or tax-free. One example of this would be life insurance proceeds. When you receive life insurance death benefits under the current tax code, they're entirely tax free, (provided your estate is under a certain amount). Also, municipal bonds are currently not taxed by the federal government, though they may be subject to state and local taxes.

In summary, the way you manage your income using these accounts can mean paying more or less in taxes. It's up to you to do. Take it from Judge Learned Hand:

"Anyone may arrange his affairs so that his taxes shall be as low as possible; he is not bound to choose that pattern which best pays the treasury. There is not even a patriotic duty to increase one's taxes.

"Over and over again the Courts have said that there is nothing sinister in so arranging affairs as to keep taxes as low as possible. Everyone does it, rich and poor alike and all do right, for nobody owes any public duty to pay more than the law demands."

Longevity Risk

I saved my No. 1 risk—longevity—for last.

It's natural to want to live to a ripe old age. Unfortunately, longevity carries with it the top risk to financial well-being in retirement. Why? It increases the likelihood that the risks mentioned above become reality. If you die at age sixty-two, for instance, does it matter that the market dropped 4,000 points or your life savings shrunk by half at age sixty-one? Nope. Does it matter that you didn't buy long-term care insurance to cover your eighties or nineties? Nope. However, if you live to age eighty or beyond, either of those things could cost you significantly. The longer you live, the more of all these potential risks you will likely face. That's why I believe you need to manage the downside risks of longevity through various strategies. The good news: This is in your control.

CHAPTER 3

Income, Income, Income: Retirement and Real Rates of Return

"Cash is just as good as money." ~*Yogi Berra*

In real estate, it's all about location, location, location. In your retirement, it's all about income, income, income. In this chapter, I'll talk about income: how to predict how much you'll need in retirement and how to achieve a reliable stream of it when you no longer have a job.

So, throughout retirement you're probably going to rely on those three different buckets to provide you with income. It's important that you balance each one appropriately and take advantage of each bucket to avoid overpaying in taxes. Doing so can have a significant effect, negatively or positively, on whether your money lasts as long as you do.

Many people assume when they retire their expenses will go down. After all, they won't be commuting or incurring other work-related expenses like business suits and dry cleaning. That assumption is often incorrect. While you can be fairly sure your income will go down, having more free time on your hands means you're going to find ways to spend, whether it's on your hobbies, grandchildren, travel, golf, or just going out to dinner more often. Those expenditures could even overtake what you're saving by not going to work every day. An important first step is to sit down and review what your actual current expenses are, as well as any you anticipate incurring on a regular basis in retirement. Maybe you're finally going to buy and regularly travel to that time-share in Cabo you've been dreaming about for years.

Whatever number will sustain your desired lifestyle, you'll need the assets to generate it, and not just tomorrow but five, ten, and thirty years from now. That's why it's critical to get a handle on what kinds of investments you'll need to actually generate that income reliably. When it's time to pay your bills, is guesswork useful? Of course not! What good is an advertisement for an investment touting the average rate of return over five, ten, or fifteen years? That's the past, and it's purely hypothetical. I don't know about you, but I want some certainty in retirement. When I pull the plug on my job, I want to be absolutely sure I'm not going back to work when I'm eighty, handing out samples at the local grocery store. You can't afford to guess, and you certainly don't want any unpleasant surprises down the road.

Not understanding real rates of return on investments is one of the biggest mistakes I see people make in planning their retirements on their own.

One day I met with a wonderful couple who had tried to do their homework regarding retirement income. They'd read various financial periodicals and consulted software illustrations provided by their employers and the company that managed their investment portfolio. They pretty much felt they had it all figured out. Until, that is, we started asking the basic questions: What portfolio mix were the calculations based on? What rate of withdrawal were they using? Is the income stream guaranteed or hypothetical? What about sequence of return? (If you need, revisit

Chapter Two for the overview of that concept.) The couple admitted they didn't know the answers.

I have another client who is fifty-nine years old and looking to retire in two years. He currently has approximately $800,000 in his 401(k) plan. When he logs onto his employer's benefits website, it shows what he could expect to receive if he were to retire today, at age sixty or sixty-five. But those figures are not guaranteed. Unfortunately, many people in my client's position don't know that. He's good at his job, but he's not a financial professional. Sometimes these monthly payout calculations are even presented as if they are pensions, when in reality they are usually subject to the whims of the stock market. Remember: Investment companies want to continue managing your money. In our client's case, I hope we've given him a more realistic picture, rather than discovering it two or three years into retirement.

Understanding Your Real Rate of Return

The players in the mutual fund industry often use publishing rates that are not truly earned by investors. The averages—called average annual rate of return—are reported in accordance with what the SEC, the government body that oversees securities transactions, requires. It sounds great: You may see an XYZ fund that advertises a rate of return of 8, 10, or 13 percent over a period of time. It seems easy to make a choice between these funds—just pick the best rate of return over a period of time. Some investment advisors don't emphasize just how speculative these rates of returns can be. They show clients numbers based on what specific funds have done in the past, which might suggest they can depend on getting the same rate of return in the future. You also need to understand that how an investment performed in the past cannot assure you it will perform the same going forward, and then dig deeper to understand the math behind the averages. They may not be as good as they sound.

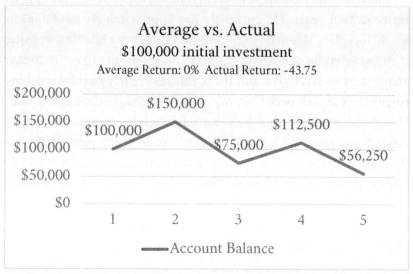

Example shown for illustrative purposes only. It does not reflect investment fees or taxes which would reduce the figures shown here.

Take a look at the chart included here. Using as an example a portfolio of $100,000, if it goes up 50 percent, you'd be at $150,000. Now the market takes it down 50 percent and you're at $75,000. Then it goes back up 50 percent. Now you're at $112,000. Then it goes down another 50 percent and you're at $56,000. The average rate of return of those years would be zero. But that's not a real rate of return, it's mathematical sleight-of-hand. The real rate of return is -43.75 percent. People don't usually understand this. They simply don't do the math, or the statements that are provided to them don't make this clear. In short, sometimes it's hard to get a clear and accurate picture even if you try to do the math, which keeps the bad news hidden.

Believe it or not, a lot of people with 401(k)s forget that they've been contributing to the plan. They'll look at it throughout four years and say, "This is what my portfolio is. This is where I'm at. Maybe I didn't lose as much, or I have made more than I thought." It's because they've been contributing month over month, adding money to an account even after market drops have depleted the funds. Many investors simply look at the bottom line, which doesn't reflect their true rate of profitability (or unprofitability).

When our team talks with investors, they almost always think their retirement accounts have done better than they actually have—until we really start digging. "Here's our portfolio," they'll say. "We've done extremely well. We're well diversified. Here's a stock that's done 34 percent or 40 percent." They forget about the other three that really haven't done well. Most of the time, they truly do not know what they earn.

An example of this is a couple who came to see me after being with their previous advisor for nearly thirty years.

We looked at their portfolio. The news was not what they expected. I gave them the facts and showed them the charts (backed by the math). They still couldn't believe it. The husband thought that I was somehow manipulating the statistics. So, I went to the internet and showed him the same results from two well-known financial websites, using their software. He still couldn't believe it. He was too emotionally invested in "his guy" to accept what was clearly true. He was making less than 4 percent on his investments. That rate itself might not be the end of the world. However, his risk exposure had led to a 50 percent loss during the Great Recession. The risk-to-reward ratio simply wasn't worth it. (And, to add insult to injury, the fees he paid his broker were outrageously high, in my opinion.)

The lesson? Don't underestimate the value of getting an independent study done on your retirement accounts. Relying on the account manager or custodial company will not automatically yield clear and straightforward information.

CHAPTER 4

The "Hash Brown" Phenomenon: Risk Allocation and Finding Your Comfort Zone

My family and I love going out to breakfast. But we are particular when it comes to our favorite dish—hash browns. They've got to be crispy and brown. Sadly, what we receive is often not what we expected. My funny (maybe a bit sarcastic) line with the waiter is "We ordered hash *browns,* not hash whites." Now there are two ways to go in that situation: suffer quietly or send the plate back with clearer instructions.

If you're thinking to yourself, "Why in the world am I mentioning hash browns in a retirement book?" Well, it's not because I think you're interested in my family's morning dining preferences. Many people have investment strategies that suffer from what I call the "hash brown" phenomenon. There's a disconnect between what they say they expect versus what their financial portfolios actually show. And all too often, they either suffer quietly or worse—they are entirely unaware of the facts.

Assessing a client's risk tolerance is one of the first things our firm does with prospective clients. When prospective clients come into my office, I almost invariably notice what they say their risk tolerance is typically does not match what investments they have in place. It may boil down to a lack of communication with the institution that handles their portfolios or it may be a previous advisor simply not following their instructions—that is, getting the hash brown order right. Yet, whether it's the waiter or the cook, the result is the same.

For example, I may sit down with couples who describe themselves as not wanting to lose a large portion of their nest egg—a smart approach, considering they are in or nearing retirement. They wouldn't want to have to go back to work to replenish those funds. However, I notice they have items in their portfolio that stand to lose (or have lost) 25, 40 or 50 percent of their value should another recession or large market drop occur.

I have also sat down with folks who describe themselves as highly risk tolerant when it comes to their investments. I ask them what would happen if their portfolio dropped from $1,000,000 to $750,000. "I would be devastated," or "I would be thrown out of the house" some of the husbands would answer. Definitely not high-risk tolerant, despite what they think. The bottom line, which amounts to the burning question each retiree and investor must ask themselves is this: "How much am I willing to lose?"

Simply put, I believe an advisor, a software, neighbor, investment manager, or broker cannot interpret your individual level of risk tolerance based on terms such as "conservative," "moderate," or "aggressive." These words mean different things from advisor to advisor and client to client. And surprisingly some will change their own interpretations depending on circumstance or market conditions! This is the reason risk tolerance needs to be plainly explained by math and data. Nobody likes surprises when it comes to losing or understanding their money. At our firm, we find it takes a little probing to correctly ascertain a client's risk tolerance. But using sophisticated research software, you can look at the factual aspects of your portfolio and your risk tolerance in a very simple illustration. You need to determine "your number," the dollar figure or percentage you can withstand losing. Of course you wouldn't be thrilled to lose anything, but there is a certain level of loss that won't negatively impact your lifestyle now or in the future. Wouldn't you agree this is the main and most important aspect? Ultimately, it's up to you to make your expectations clear and to make sure they're continuously met.

Most people in or near retirement describe themselves as financially conservative risk-takers. This is good. They probably should be conservative with most of their portfolios. What amount does that need to be? I occasionally speak to individuals who say they're fine with risking half of their portfolio, but they don't truly mean it. Could it be that they want to do a little pretending, appearing insulated and safe from volatile markets? They might say, "I don't mind a market correction of 20 percent." But when it actually happens, they get nervous. Guess what? They really couldn't handle those kinds of losses. Nor should they have to, at least not with a substantial portion of their funds.

My professional advice for most is to take a portion of your money and earmark it for a bare minimum scenario of living expenses, and guarantee it so you simply can't outlive that amount, accounting for inflation of course. Anything above that amount can be optimized and used for growth potential. In other words, set up a "paycheck" for retirement income. Then write your "playcheck." If you want to buy a second home or take the entire family on vacation, that comes out of the "playcheck" money, never from the money specifically earmarked for your living.

Another aspect I bring up in the meeting is that the purpose of money dictates where you put it. What does that mean? Some examples: If you purpose an amount for a reliable, consistent income for life, then guess where it needs to be—in a financial product that can produce those characteristics. If you want to buy a boat in three years, then the appropriate liquidity and growth for three years would need to be applied to that.

Many clients I see for the first time have failed to take this initial step. Instead, they tend to sit at one extreme or another with their money as a whole. One group has a majority of their funds invested in volatile stocks while the other has it nearly all tied up in low-yielding certificates of deposit and savings accounts.

In that first group are many investors who, when they lose in the stock market, assume it's unavoidable—a "just-the-way-it-goes" mentality. But is losing an unavoidable certainty when you're in the market? No, that's not true. You can be in the stock market, but you simply need to participate differently. For instance, an investor might have a portfolio currently generating annualized return of 8 percent per year, which most would not be dissatisfied by. However, an analysis of that portfolio, using available tools, might show that the same portfolio dropped nearly 50 percent during the Dot-com Bubble of 2001 to 2002 and the Great Recession of 2007 to 2008. This would suggest that when or if the next recession or large market drop occurs, the investor might expect this kind of loss to occur again. Granted, no two markets are the same, just as the cause for a decline is never identical. Past performance doesn't and cannot dictate future results—a needed disclaimer. But the question, which again only *you* can answer, is, "What amount of return do I desire, and how much am I willing to risk for it?"

Key: Make sure that you know 1) your potential upside, and 2) your risk factor.

It's also very difficult to fund a long retirement if you're like the second group that errs on the side of short-term, low-yielding investments like CDs and money market accounts. Remember that inflation risk, the "silent threat." If an investor is allocated heavily in these types of investments, they will be protected from market risk and it may seem like a winning strategy, yet they could eventually lose the war of attrition that inflation can cause. Clearly there needs to be a balance.

By discussing these matters in depth with an independent financial advisor, you can find the risk level appropriate to your situation. And with a little more work, you can get your "hash browns" just the way you like them each and every time. Just as an exercise, think in terms of retirement even if you're years away right now. That will give you insight into how you can expect to think in the future, and thereby plan accordingly.

To better understand where your comfort zone lies, take a few minutes to really think about your answer to the following page's eight questions regarding your financial goals, risk tolerance, and time horizon. And be honest! Although it's not nearly as in-depth enough to be used in a financial meeting, it gets you thinking and accustomed to what's needed to begin working in the right direction with your retirement dollars. Getting to know what kind of investor you are by defining yourself with real numbers instead of terms, you'll be making the first step in finding your comfort zone.

The following quiz should help you gain a greater understanding of your temperament as an investor. With this knowledge, you can select the corresponding strategies and investment types that are appropriate for you.

Investment Quiz

Goals	1. I don't need a fixed amount of investment income	Agree/Disagree
	2. I consider growth to be more important than income	Agree/Disagree
	3. I can withstand short-term swings in the value of my account in exchange for potential long-term gains	Agree/Disagree
Risk Tolerance	4. I am willing to give up a fixed payout for the chance to earn a potentially higher payout	Agree/Disagree
	5. I am comfortable holding onto an investment even though it drops in value	Agree/Disagree
	6. I consider myself to be knowledgeable about the risks and rewards of stock market investing	Agree/Disagree
Time Horizon	7. I am comfortable with an investment that may take ten years to provide the returns I expect	Agree/Disagree
	8. I don't need to depend on my investment portfolio to meet my current income needs	Agree/Disagree

Scoring: Give yourself 5 points for every "Disagree" answer and 10 points for every "Agree" answer.

40-50 points: You are a relatively low-risk investor. You are most concerned with preserving your current income. You are not willing to risk your capital for greater potential returns.

55-65 points: You are generally conservative, but you recognize the need to consider growth-oriented alternatives. You may be willing to take on a modest amount of risk to earn above-average, long-term returns.

70-80 points: You may be relatively high-risk investor. You are mostly concerned with long-term appreciation, and you may be willing to take on more risk to earn greater, long-term returns.

CHAPTER 5

Why Are You in the Market?
(To Make Money? Or Keep What You Have Made?)

A client we'll call Bob attended several of my seminars on retirement planning. It was so satisfying, albeit surprising, to see that Bob had accumulated and kept handouts, graphs, illustrations—items he received from attending over a span of fourteen years! He was "checking me out," if you will, during all that time. In fact, when we finally had our first one-on-one meeting in my office, he brought one of my newsletters from 2002! I was shocked, not only that he held onto it for so many years, but that it had taken him that long to decide he needed to make a change. He told me what finally triggered it was that he lost more than $230,000 in his company 401(k) in one month! He was finally desperate not to lose any more. It was keeping him up at night, adding unnecessary stress to his life and his body. At over seventy years old, the stress simply wasn't worth it, nor was it healthy. His wife agreed.

Bob had worked for a pharmaceutical company, plus a second company that was a spin-off of the first one. He had 100 percent of his money invested in the two company stocks that had performed very well since he started working there. About two weeks before coming into our office, the stocks dropped because one of the companies didn't get needed FDA approval for a popular, heavily used drug. Bob worked there for forty-five years and never took home more than $38,000 a year. Losing that kind of money was devastating. In his mind, that was over two decades of retirement savings down the drain. I vividly recall him expressing his concern to me: "What good was it to have those stocks if I don't have a way of keeping some of these gains throughout the years?" It's as if Bob read my mind. Here he had a purpose for saving and an investment simply did not meet his goals. Very few, if any, truly get it like Bob did. Isn't it true?

"Why are you in the market?" is one thing I ask all who come to meet me. They will say it is to make money, or something along those lines. My next question is, "Is it just to make a gain, or is it just as important to keep a gain? And then once you keep it, what do you do with it?" It's surprising how many people haven't thought this through as they move toward or through retirement.

I will concede that making money is important. But, isn't it a truer statement that we're all in the market (long-term) to *keep* money? If you don't have some type of mechanism or strategy to capture some or most of the gains you have achieved throughout the years, couldn't we conclude it's a useless exercise? Think about it: A business can make money, lots of money. But we remember some big names that went bankrupt—Pan Am, Lehman Brothers, Enron, Blockbuster Video, to name a few. For wildly different reasons, all these companies did not keep their money, despite dominating in their industry at one time or another. Would you not agree that your retirement savings plan has some similarities to running a business?

Does this approach represent a major shift in the way you look at your retirement? If it does, you'll enjoy continuing to learn more about this ideology. If you've already come to this conclusion on your own, that's excellent. Be sure your goals match your actual strategy!

Another way to look at this idea: "Don't be caught naked." In the financial world, being naked simply means you don't have any strategy to protect you from losses or ensure you don't give back all your gains. Stop-losses and tactical management are some examples that give the ability to convert to fixed income in severe market uncertainty and turmoil. Not surprisingly, Bob wanted to rid his retirement years of financial volatility and sleepless nights. He was done with the roller coaster.

When you make money on a stock or a fund or any type of appreciating asset, you want to keep that gain—the main purpose of any investment. But once you've made the gain, how do you keep it? Don't you have to sell in order to realize the gain? But once you sell that asset, now you've lost the ability to get further growth. This creates something like a "paddling" mentality, like someone trying to head upstream by bringing their oar in and out of the water. A lot of work and stress for the gains realized.

Traditionally, many people handle their investments something like this: You invest in a mutual fund. When it goes from $25 to $50 a share, you sell it, figuring you beat the market this time. Now you have your cash. But then what? How do you use that profit to derive income or growth for future use? Many people put it back into that same volatile market environment that made their gain possible, exposing it to risk that could wipe it out this time around. That's the tricky part to investing, especially when you're in or near retirement. You have to reduce or even eliminate that cycle of risk.

There's a lot of so-called accepted wisdom about "investing intelligently" thrown at us by financial magazines, blogs, TV shows, and pundits. A lot of it isn't quite accurate, in my opinion. Often, we hear it from brokers or investment advisors during downturns, when they're trying to calm us down after we've had a loss in a market drop. We're urged to "hang in there!" and told that what goes down, will come up—we need to stay in the market "for the long haul" if we want to make money. I've heard of advisors saying, "Well, you only lose if you sell," or "Those are only paper losses." Are they? If they are only paper losses, then they were only paper gains, so what's the point of investing in the first place? At some point, those paper gains have to be captured to make the whole exercise worthwhile.

Leaving Las Vegas

Here's another question I ask clients: "Would you gamble your life savings in Vegas?" That question may sound absurd, but in effect it's what some investors are doing in the stock market, right? Let's say you've got $100,000 in a bank and it's earning 5 percent interest. You know it's safe, you know it's predictable, but 5 percent isn't a very exciting return. So, you take that $5,000 you've made in interest, put it in your pocket and head for Vegas. You sit down at the roulette table and you put the whole sum down on black. Black comes in. Congratulations! You've doubled your money. Now you have $10,000. You get back on the plane home, head for your bank and deposit it. You've made 10 percent. But ask yourself: When you were in Vegas, how much of your money was at risk? Just that $5,000. Was your $100,000 nest egg at risk? No, because you left it safely in the bank. You knew better than to take it to Vegas!

So why would investors, including retirees, go to the market with their entire nest eggs? Both Vegas and Wall Street seek to entice people to bring them money. Chances are we've all heard their advertisements and promises of profitability. Yet, neither truly offers any assurance that you're going to get that money back. That's the tradeoff when you want gains in the double digits, to "make it big." So, while you definitely would not take your life savings to gamble away in Vegas, are you doing some gambling with it on Wall Street? A good gambler knows his game and tries to get rid of as much chance as he can. How well do you know your game, or strategy in the market? Have you eliminated as much chance as you can? These are important questions to answer.

Here's an example that dates back to the Rockefellers in the late 1920s. When many people lost everything in the stock market, including them (or the portion of their wealth outside or oil and other ventures), they did something a little different after that. The Rockefellers kept their principal safe and got aggressive with the yield, or interest. So think of it like this: As long as you don't "kill the goose" (your principal) you always have the future years to potentially make a gain or profit from your nest egg. That's why it's important to employ strategies that will aim to keep a reasonable portion of your money protected in retirement.

ROCKEFELLER STRATEGY

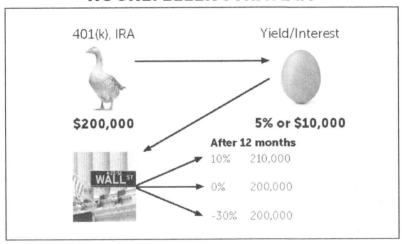

People often say, "The market always comes back, so if I stay in there long enough, I can regain my losses." That's sometimes true. But it's more like a half-truth. Let's consider some examples of how that has actually worked. (Again, this is assuming you don't need to rely on your life savings for reliable income, and truly have the ability to "wait it out.") Look at this chart of the Dow Jones Index, highlighting the twenty-five years from October 1928 through 1954 that the index took to recoup its losses.

Source: MacroTrends Historical Data

That was a long time ago, you say. So, let's move forward in time to the next chart, showing the Dow Jones from 1964 to 1982, again staying flat. What if you retired during that era and were heavily invested in the market?

DJIA 1964-1982

Source: MacroTrends Historical Data

The next chart is something closer to our day. This chart covers the years 1997 to 2018. First, look at the years 1997 to 2000. This period shows incredible gains made during the tech boom driven by dot-coms. The S&P 500, an index representing stocks of the 500 largest companies in the United State, shot up 106 percent. However, it then plummeted to about its 1997 level, erasing almost all those early gains. It took six years until 2008 to get back to those year 2000 highs, gaining 101 percent. Then as we all know, the Great Recession hit in 2008 and 2009. The S&P 500 index dropped some 57 percent, remarkably to a point lower than 1997. It took another four years to return to your peak of investment value. Therefore, from 2000 to 2013, an investment would have the same value but be thirteen years older.

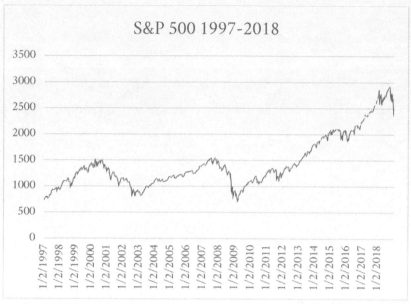

Source: MacroTrends Historical Data

Imagine a broker or advisor telling you, the client, in 2000, "Hey, I've got this great investment, come with us. You're going to be happy you did." Fast-forward eleven years and the broker says, "You remember that $100,000 you gave me? Well, great news it's still worth $100,000!" He's really hoping the conversation doesn't get steered in the direction of the management fees the client has been charged along the way. "We're in it for the long haul!" "Hang in there!" "These are only paper losses!" Have you been taught or told these canned, rehearsed responses to losing money in your account? Would that have been enough to reassure you?

Just to be clear, there were significant gains from 1997 to 2000, during the Dot-com boom. But did most investors have a strategy to capture some of gains along the way, before the Dot-com bust? Remember, that's the purpose of investing, to *keep* the money, not just *make* the money.

And finally, here's a chart of the Nikkei 225 Index—Japan's chief stock market index—that covers the years from 1989 to 2014. It still hasn't recovered from its losses in 1989, even as of this writing in 2019.

Nikkei Index 1989 to Present

Source: MacroTrends Historical Data

To cite the most recent example: In the Great Recession of 2008 to 2009, many people lost a lot of money in the market. Granted, many investors who were in a financial position to "hang in there"—those not needing income generated by those assets—recovered five to seven years later. However, they lost the opportunity to make gains with those assets during the same period of time. If you were just a buy-and-hold investor, as we're always told is wise, you would have broken even and no better. Why not opt for better?

The point is, this kind of volatility happens and is going to continue to happen. The ups, the downs, the uncertainty. If you're in your thirties, you've got some time to weather these kinds of ups and downs. But the people we work with are usually within a five-year window of retiring and don't have the luxury of hanging on for the long haul.

During the Great Recession, as in other market downturns, people who watched 60 percent of their life savings disappear in less than twelve months were told by their brokers to "hang in there." But why? Consider the source of the advice. How do advisors and brokers get paid? It's either commissions from buying and selling funds or a fee based on a percentage of the money they manage. So, if you "hang in there," they don't lose accounts. It's a business.

Peter had inherited a large lump sum from his family and was well off. His goal was to leave the lump sum intact and live off the interest. Simple enough. He'd always felt this was not really "his" money and it was important to him that he leave his children an inheritance just as he received it. However, his financial advisor/broker, who had been a family friend for years, didn't appear to have the same appreciation for Peter's money. His portfolio consisted of accounts that didn't have any protection against losses while he was living, only if he died. Some plan! The financial professional didn't have any provisions to ensure that Peter would have the income to last throughout his lifetime. By the way, Peter was just sixty years old.

Peter had started with a portfolio of over $1 million. He wasn't asking for much. He hoped to get $4,000 a month out of his portfolio to live on for the rest of his life; however, when I met him, his portfolio consisted of $600,000 in variable annuities. Added to that was the fact he was paying over $10,000 per year in fees. At the time, he was in effect paying money to lose money!

Unfortunately, Peter lost in the neighborhood of $400,000 in the Great Recession of 2008 to 2009. Despite still having considerable assets, Peter was living on borrowed money. His broker had set up a margin account—in which an investor borrows money to buy securities—to fund his monthly income. This sounds like a great strategy . . . until the market collapsed. Not only was Peter now paying almost $8,000 a year in margin interest but because the market had dropped he was actually paying interest on money he'd already lost. Coupled with the fees, this was getting expensive before he could even pay himself.

I'm certainly not suggesting that stock market investments never pay off. They can! But, as Peter's story shows, you can't rely on them solely for income during retirement. If one of your stocks is an asset that you can afford to lose, you can let it go for thirty years and see what happens. But if you need gains from those assets to pay your bills, it's just not a practical strategy.

What I tell my clients is: "You've done your job. You've worked thirty, forty, fifty years. Along the way you've invested as you've been told. You saved a part of your paycheck for years. Good job! Now here you are at the finish line of the accumulation phase of your life. You're not in your thirties and your portfolio and planning techniques must match that. You're moving to the distribution phase. Should you really be subjecting yourself and your nest egg to this level of risk? This poses a significant obstacle to your income plan."

Take Away

• Get clear on what you are really keeping. Don't base it on what you're told or what advertisements claim an investment is making.

• Don't let a long-standing, comfortable relationship with a broker or advisor stop you from looking critically at what's being done with your money. Mixing emotions with money is a bad idea (and something the wealthy rarely do).

CHAPTER 6

Why You Need a Financial Stress Test

Just recently, after doing some additional personal estate planning, I decided to increase the amount of my life insurance to create a tax-free guaranteed income for myself and family when I'm long gone (more on that planning strategy later). The insurance company sent a nurse to our house. Part of the exam involved a stress test. Before agreeing to protect me for several million dollars, you better believe they wanted to know the condition of my ticker. So they hooked wires to about ten spots on my body and put me on a treadmill.

Now, do you think they set the treadmill on zero incline at one mile an hour and asked, "How is that, Mr. Niemczyk, are you comfortable?" Of course not. They cranked up the incline to max and turned the speed up as high as it could go (at least that was what it felt like). The purpose of the test was to detect if any weakness or irregularity existed. Would it not be valuable to have a similar examination done on your investments, to see if they can withstand the stress of the next unpredictable economy and crisis? When (not if) the next market correction or crash hits, what would the worst-case scenario for your portfolio look like? This is particularly necessary to know if you plan to trust this money to carry you through retirement for life!

A good investment strategy should accomplish three things: protect your principal, give you a reliable income for life, and address inflation. Yes, you read this exact same thing in the introduction, but it's worth repeating.

To see whether a strategy is likely to do those three necessary things, a portfolio stress test should illustrate the absolute worst-case scenarios the market can experience and ascertain whether the client's lifestyle and emotions can handle the results. That information can help you and your advisor zero in on the investments and strategies best suited to you, including options like loss insurance or preset sell orders that kick in long before the market bottoms out. The results of the portfolio stress test might call for an automatic (and automated) move to fixed-income investments like bonds when the market experiences a certain drop. Or it might suggest an automatic move to contractually insured vehicles when assets reach a certain level in order to help protect against downside loss and realize gains.

It's a much better strategy than quickly deciding what to do when the guy in the next cubicle tells you the market is crashing.

Our firm bases its stress test on facts, not assumptions or sales gimmicks. We use sophisticated software that is easy to understand. Most receive a three- to twenty-page report, depending on their level of interest in the details. In other words, some simply want to know what time it is while others want to know how the clock is built. I believe all of us should expect any advisor competing to manage a portfolio to provide us with this in-depth report from time to time.

Consider an example analysis of the hypothetical client, Christopher. He has 49 percent of his assets invested in equities, held in an IRA. It has averaged earnings of 5.6 percent a year. But in another downturn like 2008 to 2009, our modeling suggested it stood to lose as much as 46.88 percent of its value. The potential upside is a decent rate of return, but not enough to justify the potential downside. The next image shows how Christopher's assets could be adjusted to leave a maximum 8.62 percent drawdown—much more in line with most retirees' comfort zone.

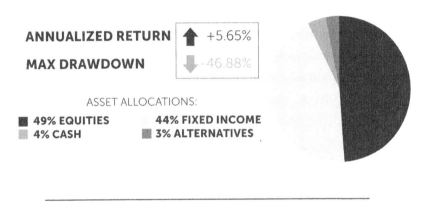

Examples are hypothetical and shown for illustrative purposes only and are not guaranteed. Your actual results will vary.

Maybe you're willing to accept a 12 percent possible loss, or maybe you're not even happy with a 6 percent loss. Either way, your advisor should be able to adjust as if your portfolio had a sliding scale of risk to align it with your personal or family risk tolerance. There is a slight margin for some divergence, but you get the point.

It's been relatively easy to make money in the market in recent years, with low interest rates, an unprecedented influx of cash into the monetary system, and tax law changes. The real question for retirees now is: How well you are protected from the downturn? China's economic slowdown, Great Britain's exit from the European Union, Donald Trump's election as president, trade wars, future tax hikes, a world-wide currency crisis, an enormous inflation or deflation event—our stress test runs your portfolio through the same types of events that have already taken place in recent years. Do you know the possible impact? You should.

Did you know there's a non-individual entity that has a similar strategy to retirees? I'm referring to an endowment fund. An endowment is a fund used by large institutions such as museums and universities to secure principal and only pay out a small portion, about 4 to 5 percent per year, that goes to campus operations and programs. Endowment investments have several goals: 1) to grow the principal, 2) to not take on too much risk that will jeopardize their future, and 3) to generate income; reliable, consistent income. Interesting, right? Institutions like colleges and universities invest in funds and companies that they feel will be successful and turn a profit, investments that are intended to contribute to both the growth of the principal and the income generated by the endowment. Higher education institutions are growing their share of investing, with combined college and university endowment assets estimated at more than $400 billion in the United States alone.

Using strategies similar to theirs could benefit a retiree, all the more so a retiree who has a much narrower margin for error.[9]

Listen, a financial stress test may not be a pleasant experience. Some have told me they'd rather get a prostate exam than sit and discuss finances for an hour. It will probably cause you to think hard about making some changes! Yet, it probably wouldn't be effective if it didn't bring some level of discomfort. It's a little like the old saying about boats: Do you want to find out your boat has a hole in it while it's docked or when it's out a hundred miles from shore? Like the stress test I took for the insurance company, a financial stress test simply is not supposed to be a "walk in the park" or something that does nothing but bring praise and adulation for your vast fortune.

Far too many people fail to stress test or fail at their stress test. Both paths lead to the wrong kind of outcome.

Take Away

• It is imperative you have your portfolio stress-tested now and periodically throughout retirement. Know what your risks are, and how rebalancing may eliminate or lessen them.

---

[9] Powershift.org. "Endowments: What Are They and How Do They Work?" https://powershift.org/campaigns/divest/endowments.

CHAPTER 7

The "4 Percent Rule:" Does It Still Hold True?

Before the last big recession, retirees were told they couldn't go wrong if they just abided by the "4 Percent Rule," meaning that if you have invested in the right stuff—mostly stocks and a generous portion of bonds—you can withdraw 4 percent from your retirement accounts each year, you'll never run out of money because the annual market earnings average is above 7 percent. A lot of people subscribed to that assumption and charted their retirement accordingly. A lot of those people are running out of money.

When people come to me for a retirement checkup and assure me they're okay because they're following the 4 Percent Rule, my first question is: "How can you be certain that 4 percent annual income from a variable-return-rate investment will be sufficient?" True, if the 7 percent return you're counting on is actually guaranteed and 4 percent is sufficient income for you, then sure—you're probably okay withdrawing 4 percent and won't run out of money. That's a great place to be! But if the expected return is hypothetical or averaged, you are opening yourself to trouble down the road, and you might get stung. When the market drops substantially, you may have to reduce or shut your income off to allow your principal the potential to grow back to where it was previously. That's the risk inherent in the "4 Percent Rule."

In truth, the trusty 4 percent yardstick of affordability has been shrunk down to something more like 2 to 3 percent because of the market volatility we've had the past two decades. If you have $1 million, that usually means you can pull out about $20,000 to $30,000 a year, theoretically, without touching the principal. Not too exciting, but that's the reality. This is especially true when you consider the factors of inflation (the silent and subtle threat) and increased health care costs. I believe that a far better plan is to have your portfolio in an investment or product where the incentive is not the interest rate but the withdrawal rate: Basically, a 6 percent withdrawal rate can be much better than a 6 percent interest rate.

For instance, a client of mine was retiring from the power company. He has a nest egg with the value of about $1 million. He informed me he wanted to take out a large chunk to buy a home in Florida and use some more to help out his kids in college. Did I think that was a good idea?

I didn't.

"Think about that million dollars as a company," I suggested. "Let's say you've got a million employees, and those million employees are expected to produce 'X' amount of output. If you pare down to 700,000 employees, but you expect them to do the work of a million, you're going to exhaust them. They're going to start burning out, and fast."

The same is true of money. You're going to either have to take on more risk to make $700,000 maintain the output potential of $1 million, or you're going to have to cut back on the production you expect from that $700,000 amount. Your goal should be to allow at least a portion of your principal to generate a perpetual and sustainable income stream, regardless of market performance. Spend it now and it's gone! Keep it there, and you may be able to later spend the interest without disturbing the principal. The client from the power company, if he went ahead with his plan, would exchange a lifetime of desired income for the idea of tax savings in Florida (yes, with some time on the beach) and to pay off college debt for his kids, debt that ideally their college degrees should allow them to cover! As the financial advisor, I personally believe this is too great a sacrifice.

People often want to buy a new car or pay off their home when they retire. Within the first couple of years, people commonly spend a lot more than what their plan models have predicted. The furnace needs fixing, or the kids need help. That's fine, but what I try to persuade them to do is take it on a monthly basis. Don't take a $50,000 lump sum and go buy a car with that, because that's $50,000 you'll never see again, especially since you're putting it in a depreciating asset. It's tough for some clients to look at paying debt off incrementally as a better idea, because people who have a large lump sum are typically gatherers. They're not spenders, and that's why they have what they have in the first place. Who likes debt, anyway? Their thought is: "Debt is a cancer. Debt needs to get cleared as soon as possible."

What I explain to them is now they have to start thinking like they are their own bank. If they've got $1 million dollars, their thinking has to be: "I'm going to make 7 percent here that's secure, and I'm going to get a loan for a car for 3 or 4 percent, or I'll lease. Therefore, I'll never lose the money needed to buy the car out-right." Indeed, the $50,000 you would have frittered away will continue earning you income instead. Doesn't that sound better?

CHAPTER 8

Annuities—the Good, the Bad, and the Ugly

Yeah, I went there. We often recommend one kind of annuity over others, when it's suitable—the fixed index annuity. Here's why:

Over the last twenty years, without a doubt one of the most discussed and debated subjects is the advantages or disadvantages of annuities. Although I'm not going to write a textbook on annuities, I'll give you "the rub,"—what everyone needs to know to help in making their financial choices. Some people have read negative stories in the financial press warning consumers to avoid annuities. And, in fact, there are some lousy annuities out there. But not all of these products are the same. It's up to individual investors to look at the facts and determine whether these investments are a good fit for their portfolios. My job is to empower them, and you, with the knowledge to draw your own conclusions.

There are four basic types of annuities. All of them share one significant advantage, which is that the IRS allows your money in any of them to grow on a tax-deferred basis. Other than that, they're very different from one another in terms of their various levels of risk and upside potential.

All annuities, including fixed index annuities, charge fees and expenses, not all of which are transparent. Many costs are built into the product pricing structure and include agent commissions, interest rates, caps, spread and participation rates, payout rates, and more. They involve contract surrender charges in the early years, which could result in a loss of principal or interest. Also, when you take a withdrawal from an annuity, you will be subject to ordinary income taxes, and if it's before age fifty-nine-and-one-half you may have to pay an additional 10 percent federal penalty.

Let's dig in.

The Immediate Annuity

You know, the one Aunt Ethel bought from a magazine. It promised her that if she deposited $100,000 she could receive $500 a month for life! Aunt Ethel passed away nine months afterward and the company kept her life savings. This is the type you see today marketed in AARP magazine. "Deposit and achieve 9.7 percent in an annuity payout." That's the lynch pin: payout. They might pay you 1 percent interest (more or less, depending on the contract) over the life of the annuity and the other 8.7 is the return of your principal. People often mistake what they're told as interest, not payout rate.

The immediate annuity is the original type of annuity, going back over 200 years. It is similar to a pension in the way it pays out. You hand over a lump sum of principal and receive a monthly check over a specified period of time or over your lifetime. To achieve this, you lose access to the principal. Let's say you have $100,000, and you're getting $600 a month for life on that. If after two years you've received $14,400, but you want to take $5,000 lump-sum, there is no account to get that from. You've relinquished your entire principal for this fixed payment. If you die, the value is gone. People who have them have generally traded their principal for the assurance of auto-pilot income.

The Fixed Annuity

The fixed annuity pays a specific rate of interest into your contract value for a period of time. Let's say you've purchased a fixed annuity with $100,000, and it pays 2 percent over the course of five or ten years. If the market does better or worse, or interest rates rise or fall, you will not see that reflected in your annuity values. You're locked into a specific interest rate, so regardless of whether the economy is good or bad, you're going to get the same interest credit each year. It's worth noting that the interest rates on these are usually relatively low. They were often more valuable in the past when interest rates were much higher, and may still serve a purpose for certain consumers, but they are not generally high-earning products.

Variable Annuities

Variable annuities are investment products with market exposure. They have upside potential. When the market goes up, you can earn more. On the downside, they often involve higher fees due to investment costs. Plus, if the market goes down, you can lose part or all of your investment. There is not a floor or base amount attached unless you purchase this through an optional rider, at additional cost. People who buy into these often don't understand the extent of the downside and have a false sense of security that their money will be there because there is an insurance aspect, or annuity potential. But they're actually exposed to serious downside risk.

This kind of annuity is widely sold by brokers and advisors. You have investment choices, which purchase underlying mutual funds. But if you're risk-averse (and if you're nearing or in retirement, you should be!) these may not be right for you.

Fixed Index Annuities

Introduced in the '90s, the fixed index annuity offers the ability to earn interest tied to the performance of an external market index, like the S&P 500, without ever being invested in the market. They also offer a guarantee that you can't lose money if the index declines due to market loss. Financial companies know how to make money and insurance companies help mitigate risk. Fixed index annuities offer the potential to grow wealth and mitigate risk.

As with a fixed annuity, the insurance company guarantees that it will protect your principal from market losses. But there's a cap on what you can make each year in interest. For example, if your annuity has a 10 percent cap and the index you've selected returns 20 percent that year, the company will credit your annuity contract 10 percent. You're protected from sudden and severe drops in the market, as well as long downward trends.

CHAPTER 9

Insured Index

W hat other billion-dollar industry has goals similar to those of a retiree? This isn't a trick question. In fact, endowment funds of institutions such as universities and hospitals have goals that overlap with retirees' goals, albeit on a larger scale. Let's again reiterate what a retiree wants:

1. Principal and earnings protection
2. To keep up with inflation at a minimum
3. Reliable income for their life and their spouse's life, allowing for and accommodating monthly withdrawals during their lifetime.

An endowment fund is established by its foundation, and it invests its capital in a way that allows it to take out 5 percent, 6 percent, or 7 percent per year—whatever is needed. If we use endowment funds as an example, which the institution uses for specific needs in its operating process, we ask: "What do they do differently that you or I or a typical retiree doesn't do?" They put their money in many different alternative strategies. One of these alternatives is the annuity, and not just any annuity; many prefer to use fixed index annuities. Let's take a moment to look a little closer at the way a fixed index annuity works.

In my opinion, if you're in or near retirement, leaving most of your nest egg in the stock market is a hazardous way to go. In a typical investment account, you put up the money, you assume all the risk, and you pay fees to do it. People come to me saying, "I've worked with this advisor for years, but I've only seen token growth." In some of the cases I've reviewed, advisors and firms have made more over the course of time than their clients have. Think about it: If you're being charged 2 to 3 percent a year and you experience a significant loss in the market, you probably won't get back up to your initial investment anytime soon. But your advisor is still being paid his fees.

This is part of why it's important to place a portion of your retirement money into financial *products* that aren't invested directly in the market but are more of an alternative option—fixed index annuities are one of those products you can consider. While a fixed index annuity is by no means a "cure-all," it can be a powerful tool in the arsenal, and something to consider as a part of a comprehensive retirement portfolio.

As I wrote earlier, fixed index annuities are *not directly* invested in the market, but they *follow* a stock market index. Stock market indexes are just ways of measuring what we collectively call "the market." The Dow Jones Industrial Average is an index that measures the average value of the stocks from thirty large publicly traded companies selected by the editorial board of the Wall Street Journal. The Nasdaq Composite Index takes the average of national and international technology company stocks. Perhaps the most popular index is Standard & Poor's 500 Index, or the S&P 500. It measures the average value of 500 stocks from businesses in different industries and is seen as a good gauge of the broad U.S. market.[10]

You can't invest directly in any of these indexes, whether by an annuity or mutual funds—they are just used as measurements, a

---

[10] Investopedia. "Market Index Definition." https://www.investopedia.com/terms/m/marketindex.asp.

ruler for showing what a specific collection of stocks is doing at any given time.

Fixed index annuities receive interest credits based on the positive growth of indexes such as these. The S&P 500 is a fairly popular one to use for this example. The contract may stipulate a cap, meaning the fixed index annuity will receive a credit representing a portion of the index's growth. It may also be based on a spread, meaning the market index must have positive growth past a certain point before the contract receives credit. One of the most powerful features is that the contract won't lose any past credit (or growth) or principal when the stock market and their respective indexes experience losses, but it also won't see any growth.

Basically, at the end of each crediting period (typically twelve months), whatever your contract's new value is will then become the new floor—the new principal moving forward. This is often called a "rachet-and-reset" feature.

Let me give you an example and let me stress that this is an example only. There are many, many different companies that offer many, many types of crediting options and caps. Please refer to the specific contract of each company when dealing with these accounts and do your due diligence.

Take a look at a hypothetical fixed index annuity with a rachet-and-reset feature using a $200,000 premium. The premium is represented by the lightest gray line that stays flat. Even if the market tanked in every year on this chart, the account's value would retain that $200,000 base. The mid-shade gray line represents a fixed index annuity contract, credited interest based on the S&P 500's performance, up to 50 percent of the indexes gains. The darkest line represents the actual S&P 500 performance. Although you can't invest directly in an index, you can purchase exchange-traded funds that directly track the S&P's performance.

In a year where the market jumps 26 percent as it did in 1998, the fixed index annuity contract will receive a credit of half the actual growth, or 13 percent. A year later, when the market again climbs 19.5 percent, the fixed index annuity will see another half, or 9.75 percent.

You may be thinking that by halving your credits you are giving up too much of your growth. However, when 2000 comes and the S&P 500 posts a 10 percent loss followed by a 13 percent loss followed by a 23 percent loss, your contractual value would have just stayed steady instead of dropping like the market did. Why is it a contractual value? There is a limit to how much interest you can earn because the insurance company is protecting you from those losses. If you would have been retired at that point and had an investment that performed similar to the S&P, you would have experienced real losses. And that's a problem when you have real bills and are counting on that income to pay for them.

Back to the chart: Notice how that FIA line stays the same from 2007 to 2009. You didn't lose like the market, but that's still three years of no growth on your account. If you were taking money out of this account for living expenses, it was going down. However, for a fee, it's possible to add a rider to FIAs accounts, guaranteeing a certain rate of return between 4 and 8 percent a year from which to take an income at some point in the future (monthly, quarterly, or annual income). This annual compounding growth rate is under contract to continue regardless of what the economy does. This is another beneficial feature of what we like to call "hybrid" annuities.

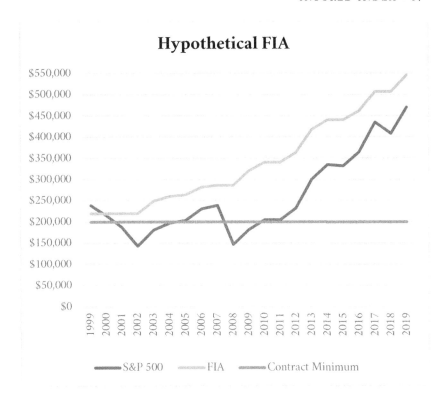

Hypothetical FIA

S&P 500 — FIA — Contract Minimum

This chart represents past performance only of a hypothetical FIA and the S&P 500 index and may not be used to predict future results. The $200,000 line assumes no interest credited in all years. Your actual results will vary.

While the S&P-like investment may at some points be worth the most on this chart, consider all the dips and dives along the way. In 2008, how are you to know the market is about to start its recovery? In 2015, how do you know the small market dip isn't the beginning of a long decline? These are fine places to be when you won't need income from those assets in the next few years.

When a client comes to our team, the No. 1 topic of discussion is how much guaranteed income they will need from their portfolio to support them in retirement. Most retirees may be tempted to reason, "If I'm averaging a 6 percent annual rate of return, I can simply withdraw 5 percent off the top, also allowing 1 percent in fees (provided they are actually paying such a low fee, which is doubtful). My account will stay the same, my principal will remain untouched, and all will be left to the kids . . . happily ever after." But the question remains, how can you possibly base a reasonable expectation of income on an unsteady, unpredictable market? The answer is you can't.

All too often, the No. 1 objection you may have regarding these types of strategies is that you are giving up too much of your growth, and it's simply not worth it. Some people will tell me, "I don't want to give up part of my gain in the good years if I use a hybrid, or fixed index annuity."

Yes, that is one downside to this strategy. However, in an investment you're not realizing all the growth of the index in the good years, anyway.

Let me explain: Consider what's in a typical, diversified portfolio. Let's take that same $200,000, and assume they have a target retirement fund which could be represented as 50 percent in stock mutual funds, 25 percent in bond mutual funds, 10 percent in money market accounts, 10 percent in real estate investment trusts (REITs) and 5 percent in precious metals. If the stock market goes up 10 percent, what went up in the portfolio? In this example, only the portion tied to the stock market. The bonds, money market, REIT, and precious metals didn't rise 10 percent. So, in your typical, diversified portfolio in this example has also not realized 100 percent of the stock market gains. Why? Because only 50 percent of your money was in the stock market.

And yet, their portfolio is exposed to downside risk. Therefore, you may reason, "If I'm going to give up a portion of my gain here, I might as well get insured and contractually guaranteed not to lose a dime on what I've made."

That's the beauty of these insured indexed contracts. Every twelve months (although some crediting periods can go to thirty-six months), you lock in whatever gains have been made, whether that's a 2 percent gain or a 15 percent gain. Whatever it is, it's taken off the table—locked in for good like a new starting principal.

I would recommend that people learn more about the benefits of these accounts. There's been a tremendous amount of "negative press" from the big brokerage houses, for obvious reasons. But, interestingly enough, some of the most vocal critics of annuities actually hold stock in the insurance companies that sell them—which tells you something about their level of understanding!

If you're in need of a reliable, consistent income, then having your retirement nakedly relying on the stock market's performance is a very hazardous way to go.

CHAPTER 10

Mutual Funds and ETFs

As an investor, you may be looking for ways to put your money into stocks, bonds, REITs, metals, etc. Two options to consider are mutual funds and their investing cousin, exchange-traded funds, known as ETFs. Both are baskets of stocks picked by a professional. Mutual funds set their price once a day and are overseen by fund managers. ETFs trade all day on an exchange, so it's easier to move in and out of them.

ETFs are designed to mirror an index like the S&P 500, which is a diverse group of 500 stocks, everything from American Airlines to Facebook to Nike. So when the S&P goes up, so will your ETF, and vice versa. On the other hand, mutual funds are usually actively managed, so the baskets might change frequently as a manager buys and sells stocks in specific areas, like emerging markets or tech.

You can buy mutual funds through a broker, a financial advisor, or directly from a fund company. ETF shares trade on an exchange like the NASDAQ or the New York Stock Exchange. Which is right for you? Most people stick with mutual funds. As of December 2018, there is $17.71 trillion invested in mutual funds and some \$3.37 trillion in ETFs, but the latter category is growing at a much faster rate.[11]

Some mutual funds are losing favor with financial experts and consumers. They tend to be seen as expensive; you may be paying around 2 to 3 percent in things like management fees and advertisement costs.

ETFs can be another, preferable option. They differ in that they're a list of stocks or bonds put in a bucket, so to speak, with a lid. There are no "fund" managers. It's a closed group of commodities or bonds, so you get the diversification of an index without the cost!

With a mutual fund, if you see the market go down and want to get out of it, you have to wait until the end of the day to see the closing price. With ETFs, there are opportunities for stop-loss management, which is a limit you set that triggers a stock being sold if it drops to a certain price point, and tactical management, which shifts an investor's fund to a more conservative position if it drops to a certain point (tactical management can work in the opposite direction, as well). Both of these options help investors from going down the road of the "lost-cause fallacy"—the feeling that when an investment shrinks we either have to add to it or wait until it rebounds before selling. As stated elsewhere in this book, market decisions are best not made in the heat of emotions stirred by a huge swing, but rather based on parameters given careful thought ahead of time.

---

[11] Statista. "Total net assets of US-registered mutual funds worldwide from 1998 to 2017 (in trillion U.S. dollars)."

https://www.statista.com/statistics/255518/mutual-fund-assets-held-by-investment-companies-in-the-united-states/;

Statista. "Development of assets of global Exchange Traded Funds (ETFs) from 2003 to 2017 (in billion U.S. dollars)."

https://www.statista.com/statistics/224579/worldwide-etf-assets-under-management-since-1997/

Have you ever had a difficult time finding out what your mutual fund's underlying investments are? That is because the managers of mutual funds are only required by law to disclose their portfolios on a quarterly basis, and they do not have to produce a log to investors of the entire period between quarters. This means managers have the ability to move away from their published prospectus' stated strategy. Has Wall Street ever had a broad reputation of being trustworthy?

In contrast, ETFs are much more transparent. Actively managed ETFs are required by law to disclose their entire portfolio daily. You never need to hunt and dig for the underlying investments only to find you're looking at a two-month-old prospectus! Even if not actively managed, ETFs still have better transparency. Why? They must produce lists of securities that are used to create a share and redeem a share. It's like they're publishing a daily recipe and ingredients list for their fund. Oh, and since most ETFs track an index, you can also look at the index itself. Higher transparency often translates to a more informed investor, something sorely lacking across the industry, in my opinion.[12]

Of note, too, is the ETF's tax advantage over mutual funds. Put simply, a mutual fund's buying and selling creates more costs in capital gains tax. Mutual funds trade a lot throughout the year. And when a mutual fund share is redeemed by an investor, the fund raises cash to pay them by selling securities.

In contrast, ETFs make far fewer trades since they track indexes that don't change much in a year. This means less buying and selling, which in turn means less capital gains. And when an ETF is redeemed, the ETF share is simply passed to another investor—no selling and no capital gains. So, what does the person who

---

[12] ETF.com. 2017. "Why Are ETFs So Tax-Efficient?"
https://www.etf.com/etf-education-center/21017-why-are-etfs-transparent-and-tax-efficient.html

redeemed the share get back? An ETF can pay them in the actual underlying securities equal to the value owed, and they can even pick securities that will have the lowest tax basis, although not all ETFs work that way.

Since ETFs came on the scene in the U.S. in 1993, it has been proven beyond a doubt that they are more tax efficient. That is why in 2017, ETF purchases were over $464 billion, a $176 billion increase over the previous year. This trend is expected to continue as people respond to the appeal of this investing tool.[13]

Just as the world of technology changes and develops, the financial services field makes constant advances in areas such as ETFs and other trends and investments. The right advisor can keep you up-to-date about them.

[13] MarketWatch. "ETFs shatter growth record in 2017." December 11, 2017. https://www.marketwatch.com/story/etfs-shattered-their-growth-records-in-2017-2017-12-11

CHAPTER 11

Take My Money, Please: Fees

Retirees sometimes engage in extravagant financial behavior without even realizing it. I'm not talking about running up credit card debt or making too many trips to the casino but rather to the fees they pay the people who manage their investments. I'll share stories of three specific cases in this chapter, then go into the specifics of various fees in the next chapter.

Case No. 1

A family I work with had a healthy nest egg of about $8 million. During the accumulation phase of their life, they lived very modestly, and the income generated from that money was more than sufficient for their needs, actually double what they needed when they finally got a handle on their finances. When they came to me for a retirement check-up, they were doing so on the advice of a friend. They didn't imagine I'd be able to help them in any way, or even believe they needed help. They just wanted to get a second set of eyes on their investments and see if they were missing anything. As it happens, they were missing something: The attorney who was in charge of their investments was charging them exorbitant fees. This man had originally worked with the relative who'd left them their money. He'd been handling the family's affairs for nearly forty years and was a trusted advisor. When I sat down with them and showed them what they were being charged for management, they were astonished and turned their financial affairs over to my office.

Case No. 2

Rick, a prospective client, came to meet with me recently. He comes from a prominent family. He and his whole family had used an advisor who had been a family friend and advisor for over thirty years. Through the years, Rick suspected something was not right but could never quite put his finger on it. After attending one of my tax and retirement seminars, he came to us to get a second opinion on how his advisor was handling his money. He brought all of his account statements dating back two years with him, and we reviewed it together. In one account he had a little over $350,000. We called the company holding that account directly. This is something I recommend to anyone who feels their advisor may not be perfectly transparent about the fees being charged. It turned out, Rick was being charged four different fees totaling $12,000 a year. Another phone call revealed Rick was paying $8,000 a year in fees on an account holding just over $350,000. He was paying $20,000 in fees on a little more than $700,000—nearly 3 percent. Rick was not only shocked. He felt betrayed, as his advisor was someone his family had trusted for decades. I call this legal extortion.

Typically, we advise potential new clients against sudden moves while we complete our analysis of their finances and work up a plan to go forward. Rick was so horrified at the hidden fees he'd been paying that he demanded his investments be moved to our firm's management that same day.

Case No. 3

This case has a different ending. A woman who attended one of our financial seminars recently took us up on our offer of a free portfolio review—a second opinion, as we like to call it. After our team examined her investments, we called her back into the office to discuss our findings, which had raised one huge red flag: She was literally earning less than what she was paying in fees. She had been using the same broker for more than twelve years and hadn't made a dime. There may have been years in which a gain was made, but it had never been captured for her benefit, just churned back into losing stocks or more fees. Armed with this information, the woman ordered her broker to make changes in her investments. But she kept using the same broker, because of the long relationship they had.

Believe me, I understand and appreciate personal loyalty. But my point is, this is your life savings. This is everything you have. You're going to need to rely on it. To risk that for a relationship in which you're not getting proper advice or clear, transparent information is not in your best interest. It's like going to a doctor. Even if the practitioner is a quack, you want to believe in the person because your life is in his or her hands, so you don't ask the questions that you should ask. You want to believe. And you don't want the responsibility. But the fact is, we have to be responsible for our finances, at least responsible enough to ask questions and listen to the answers. Get beyond the natural tendency of wanting to trust, or of not wanting to look uninformed. Focus on the facts, the math. The trust will follow when you have that. Don't get sidetracked with fluff.

What are you paying in fees on your investments? If you're not 100 percent sure about that, you're not alone. I'm willing to bet they're higher than you think.

Imagine your horse is running a race with a 30-pound jockey on his back, while the horses he's running against are carrying 100-pound or even 200-pound jockeys. Who's most likely to win? Your horse, of course—the one carrying the lightest load.

Mutual funds and the fees they carry are a little like race horses. Some have 80-pound jockeys. Others have 100- and 200-pound jockeys—in other words, heavy fees. And if your fund is outside a retirement account, taxes further weigh down performance. Over the long run, this makes a big difference.

Maybe stocks in your mutual fund portfolio were up 10 percent one year. Great! But how much did you actually make? You can't forget to factor in what it cost you to get there.

That 10 percent could be cut to 7 percent or less when you subtract costs. You may think, "Well, 7 percent isn't 10 percent, but I'll take it. I'm only giving up 30 percent of what I could have had, had there been no costs." But you're not figuring in the effect of compounding (which, as Albert Einstein famously said, is the Eighth Wonder of the World: "He who understands it, earns it. He who doesn't, pays it."). Whether you're calculating interest or fees, compounding works the same way.

Let's say we begin with $100,000. You're earning 10 percent annually, but 30 percent of that goes to costs. The first year, you keep 70 percent of the gain—$7,000. But look what happens with compounding: After twenty-five years, your $100,000 will have grown to $542,743, whereas your sum would have reached $1,083,470 at the full 10 percent. You are effectively leaving $540,000 on the table! That's no longer a 30 percent loss, it's virtually 50 percent! Combine that with the fact that you as the investor are shouldering all the risk. You see why I'm not necessarily bullish on mutual funds for a significant portion of your assets.

Mutual Fund Fees

A mutual fund is a group of stocks or bonds that are bought and sold by a group of analysts. Investors are sold mutual funds as a way to protect their investments against the presumably less reliable individual stock portfolio. Nine out of ten of the people I meet with have mutual funds in their portfolios. Following are some of the fees you encounter with mutual funds, although you likely won't incur all of them.

Management Fees, 0.5 to 3 percent

These are paid to the fund that manages the investment portfolio. These are paying for the team of men and women who actually make the decisions on what to buy and sell.

12b-1 Fees

These are named for the 1980 SEC rule that authorized them and are paid to the broker or adviser who sells the fund and services the account. You thought that hefty fee was going to a team of brilliant analysts. Nope. This is one way the broker or advisor is compensated for his time and expertise.

Sales Loads

These are upfront, back-end, or level sales charges paid directly to the advisor broker and to the firm they work for. For example, let's say a fund has a 5.75 percent load or sales charge. That means if you invest $100,000, the first $5,750 goes to them.

Back-end loads, or "contingent deferred sales charges," are taken out when you take out your investment. Then there's the level load, which is roughly an ongoing 1 percent charge for the life of the fund.

Transaction Costs

These are costs incurred by the fund as it buys and sells the stocks or bonds within the fund. These costs come out of your money and are not expressed in the expense ratio. There are also brokerage commissions when the fund manager uses a brokerage firm to buy and sell the shares in the fund. This practice is controversial. Sometimes to keep its advertised management fee low, a fund will pay for investment research using "soft dollars." These are costs that mutual fund managers pay out of their clients' accounts to a brokerage firm to cover the cost of research the firm provides for a reduction in the buying and selling transactions costs.

For example, let's say the commission for a trade that a fund manager paid the brokerage firm is 6 cents per share, but it actually only cost them 3 cents per share. The other 3 cents are used for soft-dollar "research." Under this arrangement, the fund manager may now direct future trades to the brokerage firm.

This can be also expressed as turnover: the amount a fund buys and sells in its portfolio.

For example, let's say a fund with 100 percent annual turnover pays approximately 1 percent in transaction costs. A fund with 25 percent turnover would give up 0.25 percent, and a fund with 300 percent turnover can equate to 3 percent in transaction costs. Transaction costs are not incorporated in a fund's "total expense ratio." They are taken directly out of shareholder assets.

Taxes

The fund itself does not pay taxes. Shareholders who own the fund in taxable accounts (non-retirement) pay taxes on dividends and capital gains distributed by the fund. Most investors feel good when they get distributions. I believe some fund managers will sell their positions unnecessarily just to have something to distribute

to investors. This may be good marketing, but it has real consequences for investors.

Fund managers often roll management fees, administrative
costs, and marketing expenses into one package, which is referred
to as the "expense ratio." That's the fee you pay each and every year
you own the fund. However, loads, transaction costs, and taxes are
not included in this ratio. Those are separate charges. Often clients
see the administrative charge on their yearly statement and think
that $35 or $50 is all they're paying.

Variable Annuity Fees

Variable annuities are basically mutual funds inside an insurance
contract. I've described how they work in Chapter Eight. Following are some of the fees associated with them.

Mortality and Expense (1.25 to 2.25 percent, annually)

Typically, you have to know what to ask to determine if you actually pay this fee. One aspect of this provision in your account is to
protect your balance when your portfolio experiences losses, as
happens in a market downturn. However, a majority of these provisions are not triggered until you die. That's right, you must die
to get your money back! I'm not sure about you but to me that
appears to be a steep penalty.

Say you have $500,000 in your portfolio. The market has a cor-
rection or crashes and brings your account down to $350,000. If
you die, your heirs receive $5000,000 instead of the $350,000 account value. Now that may sound like an okay deal, but let's break
it down. Typically, this charge is between 1 to 2 percent of your
account value. That means that on a $500,000 account you're pay-
ing anywhere between $5,000 to $10,000 each and every year.
Now think about it from that perspective; if the above scenario
took place, how much is the company on the hook for? The

difference is $150,00. Therefore, you are paying $5,000 to $10,000 a year for a $150,000 life insurance policy.

Living Benefit Rider (1 to 2 percent, annually)

The living benefit is a guaranteed rate of return that your account will grow. Let's use the same $500,000 and say that you have elected to have this living benefit rider of, say, 5 percent, which is the rate the company is offered per that contract. It's not negotiable. This percent may be calculated using simple interest or compound interest on a daily or annual basis.

For this example, we'll use a compounded rate. Let's suppose our account has experienced five years of 5 percent compounding. Your balance would be around $638,000. But if the market drops and takes your $500,000 down to $350,000 you will have, in essence, two values in the account. One of them is $350,000. This is the amount that you can take in a lump sum if you cancel the contract. If you have surrender charges, they will come from the $350,000. The only time the $638,000 comes into play is if you're willing to take an income based on your age and a specific withdrawal percentage assigned to that balance. Once you elect to have this payout, it cannot be changed. It is locked in. If you decide to take out more than this, your payment will drop.

Sub Account Management Fees (1 to 3 percent, annually)

Sub accounts are the underlying investments you select in a variable annuity, which often means mutual funds. However, because they are within the variable annuity contract, they are considered sub accounts, so you don't own them outright. Yet, these mutual funds are where your investment actually earns or loses money. Typically, you'll have choices of five to forty different options. You can liken it to a 401(k) plan with various investment options.

These sub accounts are managed by a third party, and they charge a separate fee.

Administrative Charges ($35 to $75)

These are charges for processing paperwork, postage, legal fees, etc. Obviously, almost any kind of investment management is going to cost you something, but nobody wants to overpay in fees. Doing so takes away money you could use yourself.

A client I'll call Frank was referred to me by one of our best clients, who had pushed him to get a second opinion regarding his investments. He'd been using an advisor who was also his accountant and a good friend. He admitted he felt a little disloyal coming to see us and said, "I don't know what you can really do for me. I love the relationship we have." But he wanted me to look at a particular account with about $225,000 in it. He explained he wanted to buy a new car by taking monthly distributions out of the account. Could he do that?

Fees are one of the first things I look at, so that's where we started. To make a long story short, I called him back to the office and showed him that he was paying over $5,000 a year in fees on $250,000. He couldn't believe it. I explained, "Just by reducing your fees, you've got more for your car payment. You can go out and lease a Cadillac for $400 or $500 a month and you're not even touching your principal."

The funny thing is that, although he handed the management of that money to us, he kept the rest of it with his pal. Personally, I don't think emotional attachment should keep you from being sensible about your money, but it happens. Whether it's because you've got a long-term relationship with a firm, or perhaps because your advisor is a relative, people do make less-than-optimal financial choices based on feelings, not facts. Sometimes I suspect they're embarrassed when they see the degree to which their trust has been abused, and that's certainly understandable. But none of these are a good reason to put your future in jeopardy. Similar things happen with stocks. I've seen people hesitate to unload a stock because they are emotionally attached to it. It was left to them by their parents or is attached to their place of employment.

When I sit down with somebody, I tell them, "Our services aren't free. This isn't charity. This is a partnership. We want to make money together. But let's look at what you're paying now and how it will compare."

Pro Tips

• Get an accurate account of what are you currently paying in fees and other costs to invest mutual funds and other holdings. If you're not sure how or where to look for that information, go to your bank or broker and ask for a fund or expense analysis of your portfolio. They're not being totally transparent if they just pull up a mutual fund site on Google. That will not catch several different costs, some of which may change on a quarterly basis.

• If you don't feel like you're getting the information you need to make the best decisions, get a second opinion from an independent advisor. You can always take that information back to your bank or broker and ask them about it. If the answers you get are ambiguous or confusing, consider going elsewhere. It's your money, and your future.

CHAPTER 12

Tax Planning

I t's halftime and the Chicago Bears are up 40-0 over their archrivals, the Green Bay Packers. But the game's not over yet. So it goes with financial planning. You've worked hard all your career, you've saved, and invested money. But there's still a half to play—your retirement. And the way you plan for taxes will play a role in shaping your financial picture during that period.

Right now, taxes are historically low, and it looks like the reprieve could last for the next several years. On the other hand, if you've been paying attention to the U.S. national debt—usdebtclock.org is a handy reference—you can be pretty sure taxes could increase within the next decade. Social Security and Medicare are each trillions of dollars in the hole, to cite just two issues.[14]

What can we do with this reduction while it's still available? Several things, actually. One option is increasing contributions to our 401(k) or IRA. If you're paying 3 percent less in taxes, you could increase your contribution by that much and not decrease

---

[14] James C. Capretta. MarketWatch. June 16, 2018. "Opinion: The financial hole for Social Security and Medicare is even deeper than the experts say."
https://www.marketwatch.com/story/the-financial-hole-for-social-security-and-medicare-is-even-deeper-than-the-experts-say-2018-06-15

your take-home pay, plus the contributions are tax deductible in the year you make them. Another option is to take advantage of Roth IRA contributions. Roth contributions are not tax deductible, but withdrawals and earnings are tax free if certain conditions are met (you take withdrawals after age fifty-nine-and-one-half and the account has been open for at least five years). If taxes are going to be higher in the future, it might be logical to pay taxes on the "seed" rather than the "crop" of your investment.

Maybe you have considered rolling your traditional IRA into a Roth IRA. Consider the following example, even if it bumps you into a higher tax bracket now. Let's say you and your spouse have a joint income of $89,000, giving you an adjusted gross income of $64,600 using a married standard deduction of $24,400. Federal taxes would equal $7,364 giving you an effective tax rate of 8.3 percent. You then decide to take a portion of your traditional IRA and roll it into a Roth IRA. Rolling over $100,000 from a traditional IRA to a Roth IRA would increase your income to $189,000 for that year and your effective tax rate to 14.7 percent for the year 2019. Will the current tax rate on $189,000 be higher down the road? With current federal debt levels not projected to decrease, but instead to increase by the trillions in the years to come, it sure could![15]

Think about it this way: "Do I want to pay tax on the seed or the crop?" Taking the tax "hit" when taxes are low and letting the asset potentially grow, tax-free, from then on can be effective strategy for keeping taxes down when drawing an income in retirement.

---

[15] Kimberly Amadeo. The Balance. February 13, 2019. "National Debt by Year Compared to GDP and Major Events."

https://www.thebalance.com/national-debt-by-year-compared-to-gdp-and-major-events-3306287.

Tax Strategies—Traditional IRA Conversion to Roth IRA	
$89,000 joint income	8.6% effective tax rate
$100,000 conversion	Traditional to Roth IRA
$189,000 total income	**14.9% new effective tax rate** in year of conversion

This example is shown for illustrative purposes only.

There are caveats, of course, and everybody's situation is different, but these tax strategies are definitely worth considering.

CHAPTER 13

Social Insecurity: What You Don't Know Can Hurt You

Some months back, a woman came to see me for a portfolio review. Part of our conversation was about Social Security. She was divorced after twenty years of marriage. A person at the Social Security administration office told her that meant she couldn't collect on any of ex-husband's Social Security benefits, although he had been the primary wage earner during their marriage. I assured her that, in fact, she could. If you've been married for more than ten years to someone, you're eligible to collect based on his or her benefits. We retain a software firm that specializes in running Social Security issues, modeling different withdrawal scenarios that can help consumers make the most beneficial decisions about their withdrawals. Therefore, we have up-to-date information upon which to rely.

She went back to the Social Security office to file the next day and was again told she wasn't eligible. She came back to our firm to tell us we were wrong. I assured her the Social Security office was wrong—not us. She was eligible, and I showed her the regulation that explicitly said so. She returned to the Social Security office once more with that information in hand. They finally agreed that yes, she was right, and yes, she was entitled to those benefits.

Do you think that was an isolated error? Guess again. Did you ever hear of the reporter for a financial magazine who wanted to see if the Internal Revenue Service was consistent? She sent the same tax return to five different branches of the IRS. Three came back the same, but two came back with different calculations of taxes owed. Yes, the IRS and Social Security Administration are different federal agencies, but the point is the answer to a question often depends on whom you ask and how they choose to explain.

There are over 560 separate ways to claim Social Security benefits. In addition to the more than 2,700 rules in the Social Security handbook, there are thousands of rules to explain the first set of rules in the Social Security Program Operating Manual System. It can be extremely difficult for a lay person to wade through that kind of rulebook. In my experience, many people wind up leaving money on the table because they don't clearly understand what they're entitled to. It doesn't help that Social Security staff members are not permitted to give personalized advice. You have to present a situation to them before they can tell you about it. If you do not know a benefit exists, you cannot know to ask about it.[16]

One such example is the lump-sum terminal illness benefit. Most people know the longer you wait up until age seventy, the more your Social Security benefits grow. But what if a person decides to delay benefits beyond the full retirement age of sixty-six and then at age sixty-eight is diagnosed with a terminal illness? Under some circumstances, and only for those who turned sixty-two prior to 2016, someone in this situation can apply for the back benefits he was entitled to between age sixty-six and sixty-eight and receive a lump-sum payment. In order to receive this benefit, the terminally ill person must have filed for Social Security when he reached full retirement age or later and then suspended the benefits so that he was not receiving any benefits. If he has not

---

[16] Karen DeMasters. Financial Advisor Magazine. Jan. 10, 2014. "Many Social Security Benefits Go Unclaimed."

https://www.fa-mag.com/news/social-security-complexity-costs-money-16573.html.

submitted the paperwork to "file and suspend" (also known as "claim and suspend"), he cannot apply for retroactive benefits for a terminal illness. That's why it sometimes makes sense to file for benefits and then suspend them if you want benefits to keep growing until you are seventy. Then if tragedy strikes, the retroactive claiming will be available as an option. Each person's situation is unique, and there are advantages to working with an expert to ensure you get the benefits to which you're entitled. Again, this strategy only applies to those who have filed and suspended a benefit earlier and who also turned sixty-two before 2016.[17]

"Mommy benefits" are another often-misunderstood provision. A surviving spouse who cares for a child under the age of sixteen can collect benefits for the child and herself as the caregiver. Different rules and age limits apply, depending on whether the child is still in high school beyond the age of sixteen, but this is often available "free money" and often goes unclaimed.[18]

Even some of the better-known benefits that spouses or ex-spouses can claim can sometimes be overlooked. I believe many Americans miss out on spousal benefits because they do not know they exist. If you don't claim them, you won't get them. And don't count on the good folks at the Social Security office to tell you about them, either. As mentioned earlier, they are actually prohibited from giving advice as to the best strategy for your situation.

The question I hear most often from clients is: "When should we take Social Security?" With so many different ways to claim, the answer isn't always a simple one.

---

[17] Bob Rosenblatt. Huffpost via Next Avenue. Nov. 3, 2015. "You May Have Just Lost a Way to Max Social Security Benefits."

https://www.huffingtonpost.com/entry/you-may-have-just-lost-a-way-to-max-social-security-benefits_us_5638ce25e4b027f9b96a0ec5.

[18] Karen DeMasters. Financial Advisor Magazine. Jan. 10, 2014. "Many Social Security Benefits Go Unclaimed."

https://www.fa-mag.com/news/social-security-complexity-costs-money-16573.html.

Let's say a husband and wife have been married for more than ten years. They've paid into Social Security for more than thirty-five years, so when they've reached full retirement age, they can take each other's spousal benefit. If you've reached your full retirement age at sixty-six, you're entitled to 50 percent of your spouse's benefit. Let's say your husband is earning $2,000 in retirement benefits. Now, you turn sixty-six, and you're eligible to get $2,000 in retirement benefits on your own. You may want to consider taking the spousal benefit—$1,000—and deferring your own until you reach age seventy, because your own benefit grows at 8 percent a year until age seventy. Taking spousal benefits does not disrupt or reduce your retirement benefit. Making that choice depends on your financial circumstances. Not everybody can handle taking 50 percent less for years. You might need the money sooner. But if you don't, it can be a good.

That's why, when a client asks what the best age to file is, I tell them, "It depends." That said, none of us knows how long we're going to live; if we did, it would be easier to know when to file!

Clients considering deferment often ask, "Is there another source of income that I can take from another asset? I'm going to have to pull from my investments if that's your option." When that happens, then we have to figure out if that makes sense. If I increase my benefit of $1,500 or $1,700 in Social Security income by 8 percent each year but I can earn 6 to 7 percent on $500,000 in investments, deferring might not be a better move.

And delaying for the longest period of time isn't necessarily going to save you from some eventualities. If you have a husband and wife, and one's got a $2,000 benefit and the other has a $1,500 benefit, and the one who's getting $2,000 passes, the other spouse will receive $2,000 but they'll lose their own benefit of $1,500. Thus, your income still drops, which a lot of people don't take into consideration. Sometimes a client will tell me, "He'll be okay when I die. He'll have mine because mine's higher than his"—but he's going to lose his if you go first.

You've got to take your health and your genetic background into consideration when considering when to file. Some clients will bluntly tell me, "We have a horrible genetic history. We're not going to be around." But most are optimistic and willing to go with statistics telling us we're likely to live longer than our parents did.

About 57 percent of people take benefits before their full retirement age, if they're not working—with sixty-two, the earliest age, being the most popular age to file.[19] If you're working, you have a limit on the income you can earn without being taxed. If you're under the full retirement age of sixty-six, you'll only be able earn $17,640 in 2018. After that, you have to give back for $1 in benefits for every $2 you earn over the limit.

Social Security: Working Before Full Retirement Age

From	You will lose __	For every __	That you earn over __
Age 62 through the end of the year before the year you reach normal retirement age	$1	$2	$17,640
The beginning of the year in which you reach normal retirement age through the month before you reach normal retirement age	$1	$3	$46,920
The month you reach normal retirement age	$0	N/A	Unlimited earnings

---

[19] Dan Caplinger. USA Today via Motley Fool. June 19, 2018. "What's the most popular age to take Social Security?"

https://www.usatoday.com/story/money/personalfinance/retirement/2018/06/19/whats-most-popular-age-to-take-social-security/35928543/.

There are certainly arguments against waiting to file. Check out usdebtclock.org, which shows the national debt and how the federal programs like Social Security and Medicare are underfunded to the tune of more than $46 trillion of liability (and going up at the rate of $30,000 per second). I don't believe the government is going to eliminate Social Security, but it may find more ways to modify the program or tax it further. You really have to run the math. Do you want an 8 percent increase to your Social Security until age seventy, or might you potentially grow your overall portfolio? It's going to depend on your income bracket and other factors. Social Security can be a tax-free benefit (I think it *should* be tax-free). But what makes it taxable is its inclusion in your various streams of income.

Some people over full retirement age work so they don't need the money. In a case like that, it might make sense to delay claiming, because you're eventually going to have a higher payment. I have some clients who are still working and just taking the money out although they don't need it. I have a client, still working, who loves her job, so she's just banking it. Again, each situation is as unique as you are. That's why I can't and won't make any hard and fast recommendations without going into a client's specifics.

How Is Your Benefit Calculated?

Your benefit is based on your highest thirty-five years of employment. The amount can change every year. At the bare minimum, you must work ten years or forty quarters to qualify. Don't assume that the government has those numbers right either, in terms of what you earned. A few years back, a client of mine looked at what Social Security had listed as her earnings and realized that they were seriously underreported. It's a good thing she looked and discovered the error sooner rather than later because if you find an error, you have to correct it within three years and three months and fifteen days following the year of the mistake. If you don't have your paystubs from the employer, you literally have to go back to their payroll department to get them. Make sure they have the right records for your earnings, sooner rather than later.

And don't assume, like my client described earlier in this chapter, that the employee you're dealing with at Social Security is clear on the regulations. As in all things financial, your best protection is to understand your situation better than anyone else and act accordingly. As the Social Security Administration's own website informs readers, "Individual employees who administer the program are not at liberty to substitute their own judgment or opinion for rulings."[20]

In the agency's defense, even some of the easiest questions take time to research, and its employees probably have fifteen appointments a day. Are they going to be able to focus appropriately on you? You can't rely on it.

Be wary, too, of taking advice from friends and neighbors. Sometimes I'll have a client tell me something like, "My neighbor and I were talking and he's going to delay filing, so I'm going to delay mine, too, based on his research. He's done a spreadsheet." There are so many factors that go into it. Your situations can be completely different.

The first step in figuring out where you stand is to go to ssa.gov and set up a username and password. You will be asked some questions that only you'll know the answers to. You'll be able to check Social Security records and see what's been reported as income, as well as get an estimate on your benefits depending on when you take them. Take that information to your financial advisor and discuss your options, including how taking or not taking your

---

[20] Social Security Administration. April 2018. "Program Operations Manual System."
https://secure.ssa.gov/poms.nsf/lnx/1402501045.

benefit will impact your tax rates. Your advisor can help you make the right choice and avoid making rookie errors or missing out on benefits and leaving money on the table.

In the final analysis, nobody can tell you for certain what the future of Social Security will be and how your benefits will be impacted. As in most things, it's better to be prepared and have a great Plan B. In the next chapter, we'll discuss other ways of bringing in a regular income after retirement, apart from your Social Security benefit, that puts your income stream in your hands rather than in Uncle Sam's.

Pro Tips

• Don't base your decision to claim or delay claiming benefits based on what your neighbor, co-worker, friend, or family member has decided is best. There are no one-size-fits-all solutions.

• Know what you've earned and be sure the numbers the Social Security Administration has for you are accurate.

• Don't expect to receive expert advice from employees of the Social Security Administration. They have neither the time nor the expertise to advise you.

• Take advantage of opportunities to create your own income streams to supplement your Social Security benefits.

• Talk to a qualified advisor and get him or her to run through your specific situation and needs before making any decision.

CHAPTER 14

Pensions:
Thinking Outside the Box

As discussed at the onset of this book, fewer and fewer individuals have pension plans or defined-benefit plans. Mostly, investors have what are called defined-contribution plans—401(k)s.

If you have a pension, there are a couple of things you need to keep in mind. First and foremost, if you have the ability to roll that pension into an IRA or take possession of that pension in a lump sum, we sometimes will recommend that you do this, for several reasons. One is the ability it gives you to reinvest that lump sum. By doing this, you may achieve a couple things. One is you may have a higher monthly payout, because you can take a percentage of those assets as income. For example, if you have a $100,000 pension, you could take $5,000 to $6,000 per year and never touch your principal.

One reason investors don't feel comfortable doing this is because there's a lack of confidence. "If we take our lump sum, we have to make the right decisions when it comes to investing. We have to make sure the money lasts as long as we do. And if something happens—if I'm the breadwinner—I have to make sure this goes on to my spouse." There are many risks someone takes when they choose to accept their pension as a lump sum. Not everyone does this. They rely on the company to invest their funds and to make the wisest choices with that money for the rest of their lives. We don't always agree with this type of reasoning.

Another reason you may want to consider taking the lump sum is that you can leave the pension balance—or I should say, the lump sum that you've invested—to your children. You can't do that with a pension. Typically with a pension, you'll receive an income and, if you've made the choice to leave your spouse a percentage as well, then they'll get that. But after the two of you have passed, nothing goes to the children.

Most importantly, on top of all this, taking the lump sum also allows you to go beyond what the monthly pension allows. Let's say four years from now, you're in retirement and you've been taking your pension. You decide you need a new home, or a vacation home, or a new car. Or you simply just want more from your account than the monthly pension is providing. Too bad—your monthly pension check won't change. If you would have taken the lump sum and invested it, and if it did well, you could have easily taken any extra growth out that year, whether it's $5,000 or $100,000, depending on the pension amount you rolled over.

You can see the versatility that taking the lump sum allows. It also allows you to increase your payments. By taking the lump sum, you can help address inflation. Most pensions lock you in to a monthly payment and they keep you in that monthly payment for as long as you continue to take that. And then when you pass away, your spouse takes a cut in pay. Not only can the compounding effect of inflation significantly reduce that monthly amount you're relying on, but also if you pass away, your spouse pays the price.

Now we've explained what to do if you have the option of taking a pension as a lump sum. Some of you may not have that option. What are you do to? Well, as we mentioned, part of my goal with this book's goal is to change your paradigm, to help you think outside the box. We want to give you information that others may not have shared with you—even the folks with whom you're currently working.

If you cannot take a lump sum pension benefit, then we may recommend another course of action that can produce a similar result, if it makes sense for the client. Let's start by discussing typical pension benefit options. Most have several choices, as shown here:

Monthly Pension Distribution

	Monthly Payment (Bob's Lifetime)	Beneficiary (Bob Dies)
Life only	$2.454	$0
Life with 10-year period certain	$2,114	$2114
Joint and 100% survivor	$1,973	$1,973
Joint and 50% survivor	$2,062	$1,031

Here we give an example of Bob. Bob retired at age sixty-five, let's say, and has four different choices. If Bob were to choose life only, that would give him $2,454 per month for his life only. If Bob were to pass away in six months, his spouse would get nothing. Therefore, when you make this choice, you have to make sure you have other planning in place to account for your spouse. The second option, life with "ten years certain," would give Bob $2,114 per month. If he passed away two years after making this selection, his pension would continue to pay his spouse for the remaining eight years. After eight years, the pension ceases. Our third option—joint and 100 percent survivor—pays $1,973 a month to Bob, and when he passes, his wife will get $1,973 per month for the rest of her life. Under our fourth and final option—joint and 50 percent survivor—Bob would receive $2,062 per month. And when he passes, his spouse will receive $1,031 per month.

Options may vary, of course, depending on the company, but these are very typical. As you can see from this diagram, if you select choice No. 2—life with ten years certain—you're giving up approximately $340 per month with this choice, which totals about $5,772 per year. Now of course there are many factors for anyone with a pension to consider.

The earlier Bob dies, the costlier this choice turns out to be for his wife. If she lives another twenty-five years, she won't have any income from the pension during much of that time. The third choice—joint and 100 percent survivor—results in a difference of $481 per month between that and life only. That comes out to $5,772 less per year.

Now, one of the worst choices and probably one of the most popular options out of all plans is the joint and 50 percent survivor. It's well intended by the owner of the pension, who often is thinking of taking care of their spouse. But think about the math on this. If Bob chooses the joint and 50 percent survivor, he's only receiving $2,062 per month. That is $392 less per month than the life only. So that's $4,704 per year. Multiply that by ten years, for example, and that's a loss of almost $50,000 in income. Now, in this case, if Bob dies, his wife's benefit goes to $1,031. For her, that would be a loss of $17,776—the $4,704 that Bob lost, plus her half, which represents a loss of $12,372, When you add those numbers together, you get $17,076 per year. If she lives ten years, that's a reduction of more than $170,000.

Maximize Pension Benefits

Steps	Amounts
1. Single-Life Pension Benefit	$2,454
2. Use % of Pension to Fund Life Insurance Policy	$500
3. Pension Owner Dies	**Pension Stops—$0**
4. Tax-Free Lump Sum Paid Out by Insurance	$350,000

In the preceding diagram, you can see how a monthly pension benefit can be maximized. If Bob needs life insurance coverage and is healthy enough to qualify for coverage, he could take a single lifetime benefit only, and he receives $2,454 monthly. Right off the top of that, he would fund a permanent life insurance policy. For this example, we're using $500 per month for that. (This is just an example to get the concept across. We understand that you may not be eligible for life insurance or be able to get a benefit as high for this premium.) In this scenario, when Bob passes away, the pension stops because he chose the single lifetime option. But his spouse would receive a tax free lump sum death benefit. What are the benefits of this?

- She gets a tax-free lump sum that can be reinvested.
- She can take a monthly income off of this sum. And now it allows for more than just a monthly pension, similar to the original pension's lump sum option, increasing the liquidity and giving Bob's spouse many more options.
- She can leave that money to her children as a legacy, something Bob's pension was unable to do.

Again, if we go back to the reason for the reduction in the choices offered by a pension, why do they offer the lower amount? The company is in fact buying insurance on you! Since this strategy works for them, why not make it work for you?

What we sometimes recommend is to take that insurance policy away from the company and go to the private market for insurance. You can still have it placed reliably, you can still guarantee income for the rest of your life. You can have greater control, access, growth potential, and the ability to leave a legacy to your children and grandchildren. There are a number of items you need to consider before implementing this concept, and you should understand how life insurance works, including its fees, expenses, terms, and conditions. If this option makes sense for you, we will go through this in detail to make sure we can implement it successfully.

Now with that being said, let's say you're the type who simply doesn't trust yourself. You don't trust any investment firm or insurance company to handle your pension. And you decide to leave it there even though you have the option of rolling over the lump sum. What we want to make sure is that you request an annual funding notice. Employers are required to send annual funding notices on a yearly basis. What does the notice do? Well, the annual funding notice shows how the pension is funded and shows the value of the assets that your plan has. It shows the value of the liabilities. It should show you, depending on the company, how those assets are invested. It will show you the percentage that your pension is funded.

For example, a 100 percent funded pension is optimal. It means that 100 percent of the payouts that they have promised to employees are being met. If your pension is funded 60 percent, that means there's a 40 percent shortfall in the promises that they've made. Mind you, more and more pensions, especially in the state of Illinois (in which this book is being written and our practice is located), are experiencing significant dollar deficits in the public and private sectors. The promises that were given are not being necessarily met for many reasons. Enough assets are not being collected from current workers to pay retirees that are receiving pension, or the funds are not being prudently invested. There's a disconnect. Also, the promises they made as to paying these retirees were simply overstated from the get-go. Mathematically, they could never fulfill those promises. They simply miscalculated. What I like to point out is that, here we are in the biggest bull market in history, going on eight years, nine years of positive returns in the stock market, and if your pension is still not fully funded, do you expect it to be fully funded if or when this market crashes? Probably not.

What you also want to do is verify with the federal Pension Benefit Guaranty Corporation what portion of your pension it will guarantee if your pension plan should go into default. You can go to the PBGC website, pbgc.gov, to see how much of your pension is covered.

CHAPTER 15

Bounce Your Check
to the Funeral Home

Okay, the title of this chapter is not to be taken literally. Intentionally bouncing a check would be a form of fraud and would actually be illegal. You've conducted your financial affairs in an above-board, honorable manner all your life and have no intention of giving anybody the chance to say otherwise after you're gone. But there's a serious point behind the title. It pertains to how people handle their assets during retirement.

You (and your spouse, if married) have probably worked hard for decades, saved and invested with the goal of leaving something to your children or other treasured people in your lives. Or perhaps you do intend to enjoy retirement to its fullest, and why not? Perhaps no one left you anything and it's your right to enjoy what you have built up. No matter what your intentions are, I bet you would prefer *not* to leave it to the IRS. That's the bottom line. Think of it like this. Remember the admittedly implausible scenario where the Bears are beating the Packers 40-0 at halftime? If I ask you who's won the game, you would say, "Neither team, the game isn't over." I'd reply, "Correct." Even though the Bears are *winning* the game, it doesn't mean they have *won* the game. Similarly, your accumulation years may be coming to an end—or have ended—but you still have the distribution phase of your life, i.e.

retirement. You also have one more "quarter," which includes the need for estate planning.

Whether you have a plan or not, the IRS will make a claim as a beneficiary. The question is, just how much will you let them take? It's up to you. Just like the football game, the retirement game can be lost from taxes. Just look at a few billionaires who have died just to see their estate get gobbled up by income and estate taxes. Heirs of Howard Hughes, the inventor, aviator, and Hollywood producer, lost billions because of poor planning. When you (and your spouse, if applicable) pass away, estate taxes and income taxes can eat up 40 to 60 percent of what is left in your IRAs and other accounts you might be planning on giving to your children.

Typically, of course, children or other beneficiaries are thankful to receive what they get and might shrug off the tax losses as an inevitable fact of life. In fact, through better planning, you can legally eliminate or reduce that tax bite. That is part of what your financial and retirement planning team should do for you. That team should include an estate planning attorney and tax advisor (not a tax preparer), and should be planning ahead for your taxes, not *reacting* when you file your return each year.

That's why I tell my clients to plan to bounce the check to the funeral home. That's just an exaggerated way of saying don't be afraid to spend down your assets and live out your retirement dreams. You can still leave a hefty legacy to your children in a tax-free manner.

Full disclosure: I am not a licensed attorney or a licensed tax professional. However, I do have a good grip on the innerworkings of these planning techniques and work closely with both types of professionals in constructing ironclad legacies for clients—and there are good, solid financial reasons why you want that final check to bounce (metaphorically speaking).

Let's say you have a $500,000 IRA. You're determined to live off of the interest income, because for years you've heard the maxim, "Never touch your principal." You learned this from your parents, who never accrued any debt and lived within their means. But what happens to that carefully saved $500,000 when you pass away? Let's say you've got two children, Bobby and Susie, who are your primary beneficiaries. In this case, as long as you and your spouse are able to live off the interest, they're each going to inherit $250,000—or so they think. Your spouse passes away and leaves it to you. You continue living off the interest, then you pass away. But before it gets to Bobby and Susie, there's a third beneficiary that takes a cut first—the IRS.

Think about how income taxes work. Most adult children have careers. Let's say Bobby and Susie are each earning $70,000 a year. If each of them gets a check of $250,000, that's going to be added on to what they already make. What would the tax bracket be for $320,000? That additional income is going to be taxed at far higher rate than their normal tax bracket. A lot of people fail to take this into account, but you can bet the IRS does not. That's $100,000 they're going to lose off the top to the IRS, minimum. You didn't leave them with $250,000 each—you left them with $150,000. If you had planned better, the kids could have wound up with a much heftier legacy.

Here's one way to circumvent this scenario. Let's say you have put away $500,000, on which you're earning 7 percent. You need 6 percent to live off, so take the remaining 1 percent and fund a life insurance policy that can pay your estate taxes. Then, when you pass, each child will be left with $250,000, tax-free. You're leveraging your money, spending money each year now to leave a half-million-dollar legacy later. What happens to the rest of the principal? Mom and Dad get to spend that instead of losing it to the IRS.

IRA – BENEFICIARIES

NON-SPOUSAL DISTRIBUTIONS

IRA
$1,000,000

MIKEY ↘ ↙ ELLA
$500,000 **$500,000**

LUMP SUM PAYOUTS

MIKEY	ELLA
$500,000	$500,000
-$150,000	-$150,000
$350,000	$350,000

IRS BENEFICIARY $300,000

Example is shown for illustrative purposes only.

Before 2020, it was also possible to lessen the tax bite for those to whom you're leaving a legacy by rolling your IRA into a beneficiary IRA, allowing them to take your IRA as a series of payments instead of as a lump sum. This strategy was popular since it spread the distributions tax consequences over beneficiaries' *lifetimes.* But as of 2020, Congress has decided they would rather have the taxes from a person's IRA sooner rather than later, meaning they will limit your family's ability to stretch the IRA to a matter of years instead of decades or lifetimes. They have accomplished this by passing the Setting Every Community Up for Re-tirement Act (SECURE Act) and the Retirement Enhancements and Savings Act of 2019 (RESA). This image shows what happens when identical inheritances from an IRA are simply withdrawn.

The majority of inheritances are spent within five years of inheriting.[21] A beneficiary may want to pay off a home, open a busi-ness, or make an investment. There's nothing necessarily wrong with that, but it can make Uncle Sam into your second, unin-tended beneficiary.

Most economists agree taxes are only going to continue to go up in the future because the United States is going trillions more in the hole each year, meaning the $100,000 tax bill your hypo-thetical children would pay today on your legacy is likely to be even higher in the future. You might have done very well in accu-mulating, but if you distribute it improperly, what's the point? Just as in football or basketball, it's not halftime but the end of the game that really counts.

---

[21] Alaina Tweddale. Prudential. April 20, 2017. "Why 7 in 10 People Who Suddenly Inherit Money Lose It All."

https://prudential.kinja.com/4-smart-strategies-for-investing-an-inheritance-1794266102.

CHAPTER 16

Asset Protection

Many ways to be sure your loved ones get what you have worked so hard for requires an understanding of basic asset protection.

What do we mean by asset protection?

Well, many estates have gone bankrupt, have actually owed more than what they had due to the taxes, probate, and court costs, from bad estate planning. So, let's start there.

A couple of examples. The Godfather, Marlon Brando, had an illustrious career but no estate planning. Everything that he had built was lost after his death.

Another is Howard Hughes. He was a multibillionaire but his estate was emptied because of poor or no estate planning. You can have a wonderful life as far as accumulating assets, make double-digit rates of return, not spend a whole lot during retirement, but then at your demise your wealth can dissipate if it's not properly structured.

Let's take, for example, three of the most common ways individuals pass money to their children or other heirs. And those are wills, a revocable living trust, and a beneficiary form.

Will

Typically, anything under $100,000 that doesn't have a title will go into your will. However, more and more people feel their will is going to dictate where all their assets go. So they name certain members of their family as recipients of their estate, not knowing that the will has little to do with where the money's going to go.

Trust

Many people, perhaps including you, have revocable living trusts. You choose to spend the money and the time to hire a great legal team that puts together a living trust that details where your assets are going to be passed on to, maybe even when they're going to be passed on. You have some type of guidelines on what age beneficiaries receive it or what the money can be used for. You take care of all these sorts of aspects and characteristics when developing a trust. You go into the big criteria and figure out how the funds will be managed and all the details that your financial professional and lawyer lay out for you.

The problem is, we see many people do those things but then they don't actually pull the trigger. And what do I mean by that? Well, they create this wonderful shell that is the trust, but they don't put the assets into the trust, so they don't fund the trust. "Funding the trust" runs into the next piece of our asset protection strategy: titled assets and assets with beneficiary statements.

Titled Assets and Assets with Beneficiaries

An asset's title or statement of beneficiaries trumps your will, and it trumps your trust. If you've elaborately structured your trust, but you never transfer the title of your assets into it, then they are not protected by that trust. They will not go to whomever you choose in the structure and layout that you wish. Therefore, you've got an empty shell.

These assets could be a brokerage account or an annuity contract, real estate, etc.

So if you're feeling swell because, "Well, I've updated my will," but you never reviewed your other assets to match your wishes, you could be in for a nasty shock—or, rather, your loved ones could be—when your assets don't go to wherever or whomever your will or trust painstakingly detailed.

So, what do we gather from this? What's the takeaway? We want to make sure that your assets and your beneficiaries are up to date. Take a look at who you have listed. If you have a living trust, put that asset into the living trust, as long as it's a non-qualified, non-retirement fund or asset. There is an exception here, which is specific qualified retirement assets such as an IRA or 401(k)—you may not want to name a living trust as a beneficiary of retirement accounts such as this, because that would trigger all taxes and possible penalties to be paid immediately.

One advantage of a trust is that it has more oversight. Let me give you an example. Say you have several assets that you intend to pass on and you're looking for equitability between your two children, both of whom have been named as executors of the estate. If only one of them has power of attorney over a certain asset, they could liquidate it or act unscrupulously without the knowledge of the other executor. With a trust, because there's a little more institutional oversight, if the trust owns the asset, the institution that manages each asset will have a two-step verification of notifying both entities, because that institution is legally on the hook for being sure all relevant parties are involved in the decision-making.

IRAs are particularly tricky when it comes to asset protection. If you die and your IRA passes to a spouse, your spouse can simply roll it into theirs, put their name on it, and begin distributions—

business as usual. But with your children inheriting, if you name them as your beneficiaries, they as individuals will have one option, to withdraw from the account all assets over a maximum period of 10 years, creating a big tax burden and exposing the money to threat of lawsuits and divorce.

That offers very little asset protection from your end—you won't be able to decide whether your children take the IRA as a lump sum or decide to take minimum withdrawals. Maybe your adult kids want to pay off a home, buy into a business, buy a second home, fund their children's or your grandchildren's college, and they take large chunks of IRA money, which can be expensive. You have no type of written policy on how that money should be taken out if you simply name them as the beneficiary of the IRA. If you title the IRA to a living trust, remember, it will be dumped out as a lump sum and must pay full taxes plus penalties—this is not something I recommend.

You can't mandate any particular investment strategy when the kids inherit the IRA. Additionally, non-spousal beneficiaries of IRAs are fair game in divorce proceedings, as well as in lawsuits. In June 2014, the Supreme Court ruled in Clark vs. Rameker that benefi-ciaries are not protected from these events with regard to inher-ited IRAs. Why? Because beneficiaries, unlike the first IRA owner, did not earn or save that money.

So how can you protect these assets in case your children go through a divorce or get sued? How can you ensure that the IRA you've built up over the years can benefit not just your children, but also your grandchildren?

An IRA trust, a special kind of trust, structured specifically to handle an IRA, can put boundaries in place to protect against neg-ative life events, lump sum withdrawals, and mismanagement.

With an IRA trust, you can stipulate conservative or moderate investing approaches and be sure it gets rolled into a Stretch IRA.

I personally am not an attorney. But we have built a network and team of professionals that includes estate planning attorneys who can help with these sorts of scenarios.

The threats to your estate and assets don't appear only after your death with irresponsible heirs or a greedy Uncle Sam. They also come with expensive health crises, so it is important to plan for protection from that, as well. According to recent statistics, 70 percent of sixty-five-year-olds will need some form of long-term care during their lifetimes. Of those who enter a nursing home, 25 percent will need care for five years or more.[22] And the average annual cost for a private room in a nursing home is $100,375. It's estimated in ten years that cost will creep up near a $135,000 per year for private care. Those numbers are staggering.[23]

Many people mistakenly believe Medicare will cover those costs. Medicare covers a lot of things; it covers acute care, emergency care, urgent care, short-term stabilization, trauma care, etc. What does Medicare not cover? It doesn't cover custodial care, or what we colloquially call long-term care, when your care isn't tied to any particular health event, but affects the way you live and your quality of life. I meet many, many people who are under the delusion that Medicare will cover long-term care, but if you need care because you cannot bathe, dress, eat, move around your house, or remember safety things like turning off the stove or locking the house, that's not a Medicare-covered thing.

Medicaid, of course, does cover long-term care, but you have to be impoverished—literally meeting the government standard for low income—to qualify, or spend through your own assets

---

[22] LongTermCare.gov. "The Basics."
https://longtermcare.acl.gov/the-basics/index.html
[23] Genworth. 2018. "Cost of Care Survey."
https://www.genworth.com/aging-and-you/finances/cost-of-care.html.

until you become impoverished. If you're looking to protect your assets, Medicaid isn't your funding strategy.

Often when we think of the need for extended health care, we think of nursing homes, or "facilities," words and terms that carry an outlook that is bleak or boring, and we might free-associate with wheelchairs, hospice, etc.

Yet, there are many other ways to meet long-term care needs outside of that somewhat stark scenario.

Think about when you first find yourself or a spouse having difficulty bathing. Or maybe you can no longer safely drive. That's not a *danger*, per se. You don't need to go to a nursing home, right? Why not stay in your home? It's a beautiful home, and you have nice neighbors and it's where you are comfortable. But what about the cleaning? The grocery shopping? The laundry, home maintenance, physical therapy appointments, bathing assistance, and numerous other things you will need help with?

We need to be prepared for these eventualities. One option is long-term care insurance, a policy that would begin to pay for care (yes, even at-home care) once a doctor confirmed you were no longer capable of performing two or more regular activities of daily living. So, why don't most of us have long-term care insurance? And why are a majority of policies allowed to lapse?

For starters, long-term care insurance is expensive. And it can get more expensive as you age because insurance companies can increase the premiums, potentially pricing you out of a policy as time goes on. Also, you have to be healthy enough to qualify for a long-term care insurance policy to begin with—if you *know* you'll need care, you probably won't qualify in the first place.

One other significant hurdle is the chance that you purchase a long-term care policy and pay for it for years, foregoing other needs or wants, spending thousands of dollars, and then you never actually need long-term care? When you pass away, the insurance policy will just be money gone, unavailable to your heirs.

There are other options available to address this gap. For one, the Pension Protection Act, Public Law 109-280, courtesy of the government, allows individuals to use tax-free money from their IRA to fund long-term care these days.

As we discussed earlier, pulling money from your IRA means paying taxes on money that has never been taxed before. Yet, thanks to the Pension Protection Act mentioned earlier, we have strategies where we can take an IRA, roll funds over to a life insurance product with long-term care benefits, and then use those benefits tax-free for extended health care needs. You read that right—not tax-deferred, but tax-free. So, you take your initial investment, any of the gains, and you can pull it out, income-tax-free for health care. Now, there are many strategies to accomplish that. You may say, "Well, I only want to use a portion of my IRA to cover that need." And also, at some point, let's say down the road, you want to get a majority of that money that you've allocated back. If you decide fifteen or twenty years later, "I no longer want this long-term care coverage," you can decide to get your principal back. So, that's a great strategy to cover this long-term care need without having to break the bank.

Another aspect to the changes in the long-term care area are riders you can purchase on your life insurance policy. Let's say that you don't use the LTC benefit. Let's say you never become sick to the point where you need long-term extended health care. Wonderful! What happens to that money you paid in? The premium you paid for the rider is gone, but if your policy itself has accumulated cash value, you can take it out as a loan or withdrawal (reducing the cash values and death benefit). Or, if you pass away, that money goes to your children tax-free as a death benefit.

These policies may be easier to qualify for than a traditional long-term care policy. They have chronic illness riders on them. So the day of having only one way to pay for a standard long-term care event, in my opinion, is gone.

CHAPTER 17

DIY Investors

Many investors read financial magazines and the business section of the newspaper. They watch TV shows and peruse websites about investing and money. They figure that, given all the knowledge they have, maybe it's not worth hiring somebody.

Then there's a group—I mentioned them earlier—whom I call Retirement All-Stars. They generally stick to what they know. They don't try to make themselves into experts in every field. They simply find the best specialists they can find and put themselves in their hands. They listen, they learn, and they're not afraid to ask questions. They include people like Ben Bernanke and Dr. David Babbel, both of whom use investment advisors and some of the same strategies we employ for our clients. You probably recognize the name of Bernanke, former chairman of the Federal Reserve. More than half of his income is derived from the same kind of investments we use with our clients. Babbel is just as well-known in financial circles. He's a guy with six university degrees who has spent over thirty years teaching economics at University of California-Berkeley and The Wharton School of Business. He's the Babe Ruth of the finance world. Yet, when he put together his retirement plan, he decided not to lay it out himself, or to manage it himself. He also understood that it's important to have some of his assets on autopilot, generating a reliable stream of income he can't outlive.

I'll mention another couple of Retirement All-Stars, a man and wife with a $9 million portfolio that we manage for them. You might think with that kind of money, they'd be looking over our shoulders every second, questioning the choices we're making on their behalf. Instead, after doing their due diligence on our firm and the strategies we use, their attitude became, "Whatever you recommend, we're going to follow." Why? Because they understand it's not their expertise—in other words, they know what they don't know—and they're willing to choose an expert and trust in his judgment. That's typical of wealthy investors, and of smart ones.

I understand the strong desire of some people to keep their financial operations under their sole control. They may have been burned with bad advice from a large brokerage firm or a cookie-cutter solution from their bank that didn't really fit their needs.

Another factor that fuels do-it-yourself investing is the proliferation of articles, videos, and blogs on the internet. The information can be overwhelming, contradictory, and misleading. Clearly, not everything you're going to be told is going to be strictly true—or at least, not all of the truth.

You have to understand that the purpose of these articles is often one of two things: to increase readership or to push a certain product. But you simply can't take a single strategy or financial product and make it fit all investors, because investors come in all ages and income groups, with different goals in mind. There's a big difference between a twenty-five-year-old in the accumulation phase and a sixty-five-year-old needing an income he or she won't outlive.

Bernanke and Babbel and a lot of successful investors understand this, which is why they're not afraid to get help.

Catastrophic Loss

One last observation about Retirement All-Stars: They don't rely on chance when it comes to devastating events. Take a catastrophic illness: If a well-to-do individual becomes ill and some type of long-term care is necessary at a cost of $12,000 a month, you'll find they've already made some provisions to cover that cost. Although they could afford to pay it out of pocket, they are prudent in the sense that they have protected themselves financially by arranging their affairs to get that $12,000 a month worth of care via pre-planning and insuring against those costs. You may be surprised to know there are many options to achieve this without breaking the bank. The financial industry is similar to the technology field in that there are updates and changes for the good. The Retirement All-Stars have positioned themselves to get that kind of coverage.

CHAPTER 18

Choosing an Advisor: A Winning Team Approach

Staying informed and involved regarding your investments is important. Nevertheless, it's not usually a good idea to go it alone. In that respect, the financial world is little like the legal world: We all know what a divorce is, or what a lawsuit generally entails, but that doesn't mean we're able to represent ourselves in court. We hire a professional.

First, though, you need to understand a little bit about the terminology Wall Street uses to describe those who want to handle your investments. This basically comes down to two words: advisor and broker.

An advisor is a professional you hire to help you develop your retirement plan, pick stocks, bonds, annuities, real estate investment trusts, and other investments for you. Advisors are fiduciaries, which means they're legally obliged to act in your best interest.

Advisors usually charge a flat salary or fee to design a blueprint of your goals and retirement plan, or else they receive a cut (1 percent is typical) of the assets under their management. They may also earn a commission on whatever financial products they sell you. Because of the compensation structure, advisors are seen as having fewer conflicts of interest than brokers. They are required to be up front with you about any conflicts of interest and disclose how they are compensated.

Broker is short for stockbroker—someone working for an investment or franchise firm whose job it is to buy or sell stocks, bonds, mutual funds, ETFs, and other financial products for clients. Brokers are paid on commission: no transaction, no pay. So there's considerable incentive for them to sell investment products if they want to keep their job, and create turnover. They're not fiduciaries.

The broker's standard is "suitability," which only means "as long as the investment is appropriate for a client." That means the investment should be appropriate for a client but doesn't have to be in the best interest of the client or even conflict-free, which means it could be a proprietary investment or a product sold by the company, or it could mean it's the only type of investment sold by the company.

Broker, Employee-Based Advisor versus Independent Advisor

The standard for an advisor is that they're legally obligated to act in your best interest. There's one more distinction to be understood, between independent advisors and those who work for big brand-name firms.

How do they differ? The easiest analogy involves imagining you're going to McDonald's. If you eat there, you're going to get only what they have on their menu. In a sense, your desires are going to be secondary to that of the restaurant chain, shoehorned into the parameters it has deemed fit for you. That's how many big firms operate. An independent advisor is more like a personal chef who can prepare anything you like.

As an independent advisor, I have access to the same financial products as employees of Edward Jones or PNC, plus many more. We don't take possession of your funds. If you say, "Mike, we love what you've put together for us. It makes sense," you're not going to roll your funds over to MLN Retirement Planning. We work with TD Ameritrade, Fidelity, and other major firms, and that's who holds your money. We're not married to any one company or set of investment options, so we can offer whatever we believe will work best for you.

Also, because we're a smaller firm, I deal with the investments, while a team that we've built handles other aspects of your account. Why does size matter? Personally, when I'm doing business I prefer to deal with the owner of the company or somebody who's second or third in line to the owner of the company. I know I'm going to get better service and the best they have to offer. At MLN Retirement Planning, it's literally my name and reputation on the line.

We own a small tax firm. I'm not a tax professional, but I have the team to do it. That means we can submit a tax return through tax attorneys, CPAs, and enrolled agents. Depending on what that return warrants, if the client is heavily invested in real estate or they have a corporation or they're just an individual taxpayer, we find the appropriate team member to work on it. The attorney's job is to make sure that what you've built up gets properly passed along, according to your wishes. All of us work together to be sure that your money is working for you. This kind of one-stop shopping insures a seamless experience for you and guarantees that everybody's on the same page.

Without making a blanket disparaging statement about big firms, I will say that many of them rely too often on cookie-cutter plans geared toward accumulation, judging by the portfolios I see. Many of these plans *might* work, provided you're twenty to forty years old, favorable to risk, and fortunate enough to be living through a bull market. But they're not necessarily appropriate for people nearing their retirement and distribution phases. These are two distinctly different stages of life, and the planning has to reflect that. Don't let the name on the letterhead lull you into a false sense of security. It's all too easy to get lost in the weeds if you're a smaller investor at a big firm.

The majority of clients I work with are nearing or in retirement, so my team's focus is generally not on younger people. If people in their accumulation stage have a 401(k) or other retirement plan, we can definitely manage that for them with the understanding that it's not to be touched until far into the future. And we're happy to talk to younger clientele, but we excel in the space of true retirement preparation. A lot of information the big firms use in their marketing is geared toward accumulation. Investors sometimes get excited and want to know what the next hot stock is going to be. It's a fun topic to discuss at a cocktail party. What are the top mutual funds this year? What will the best funds be next year? All of that is fine if you're looking for pure speculation and still have plenty of earning years ahead of you. However, if you're nearing retirement, these marketing and accumulation strategies are just noise that typically don't fit what you need.

How do we pinpoint where you are and how much risk you should take? The answer starts with a careful evaluation of your investments, the stress test we covered in Chapter Seven, and our long experience with clients in similar circumstances.

How do you choose who should handle your money? Ask lots of questions, such as:
- How long have you been in practice?
- How will you position me to keep the gains I make?
- How will you keep the IRS from becoming my biggest beneficiary both during and after life?
- Do you use a team approach?
- Are you a fiduciary?
- Are you an independent advisor?
- Do I pay fees regardless of performance?

When it comes to a particular investment opportunity, financial advisor and TV host Suze Orman suggests asking: "Is your mom invested in the instrument you're recommending?

But here's the most important question of all: "How are you going to protect me against the downside?" Because it's easy to make money when the market's going up, when the economy is full of sunshine and all is well in Pleasantville. A majority of portfolios we see are all positioned for the upside, designed to profit from growth but lacking a strategy to keep the achieved gains. Rarely—maybe in one out of fifty cases—do I see retirees whose portfolios are equipped with stop-loss provisions, insurance against losses or any other type of safety net.

Don't get star-struck by a beautiful office or a famous firm's name, or by convinced by a friend who says, "I've had my money with them for forty years." Instead ask the question: "How are my gains protected?" Hopefully they won't squirm. Remember that a beautiful office doesn't mean they've made money for their clients. It means they've made money for themselves.

CHAPTER 19

Taking Charge

I'm often asked how I came to be in this line of work. I come from a hard-working family. My mother was a stay-at-home mom who cleaned houses part-time. My father drove a gravel truck and worked for an excavation company. I was scouted by the pros as a baseball player in high school and got a scholarship out of it. Everyone assumed I'd go on to the pros when I graduated from college.

It was around this time that I saw my dad struggling financially. He'd invested his hard-earned savings with a guy he'd known for a long time and he was losing money consistently. I remember hearing his end of angry phone calls with his advisor and seeing his frustration at never getting a satisfactory answer from this guy about why his money was doing so badly. Yet he just hung in there, because he didn't know what else to do.

That's when I made a decision: "I want to get into finance and learn how to deal with investments, because there has to be a way that we can logically figure this out and fix it. My parents shouldn't have to work so hard for every dollar, just to see it slip through their fingers."

Baseball paid for my first two years at college. I made All-American in my sophomore year. For personal reasons, I decided to give that up.

When I graduated I went to work for one of the big financial firms. I learned a lot—enough to know that being restricted to offering my clients a limited menu of options wasn't really the most financially rewarding approach for them or me. That's when I decided to become an independent advisor. I could see that crafting a solution to fit the individual is better than trying to shoehorn the client into something just because it was part of the firm's inventory of financial products.

I still believe the client's needs come first—and the biggest need I encounter with clients on a day-to-day basis is that they not run out of money before they run out of life.

If you take only two things to heart in reading this book, I hope the first one is: Ask questions. Don't just glance at your financial statement and assume that all's well. Don't let any broker or any advisor brush off your inquiries. If he or she doesn't make a genuine effort to clarify and justify the investment choices he's making on your behalf, you need to look for someone who will. It's your money—it's your retirement—and you can't afford to take anything you're told on trust. Don't be swayed by a personal relationship with your advisor or by the reputation or fancy offices of a firm. Insist on answers—and results.

The second thing I want you to take away is: Always, *always*, get a second opinion—and not from the same source that you got the first opinion. That should be obvious to anyone. Clearly the source of your first opinion isn't likely to change their mind or point of view. I think of another hard lesson learned from my dad, who had a painful lump on his chest for months. His doctor, whom he'd been seeing for years, told him it was a pulled muscle and gave him pain pills. Finally, he went to another doctor for a second opinion, and that doctor discovered it was a cancerous tumor. By then it was too late for my dad.

Don't make a similar mistake with your finances. Getting that second opinion can save your retirement or possibly even save your life.

If you'd like to learn more, we'd like to hear from you.

About the Author

M ichael L. Niemczyk of MLN Retirement Planning, Inc. has been helping families and individuals for more than twenty years. A licensed Investment Advisor Representative in Illinois and Wisconsin, holding the Certified Income Specialist (CIS) professional designation, Mike has hand-selected a team of professionals—including investment advisors, tax planners, and estate planning attorneys—to design, implement, and manage retirement plans for individuals, families and corporations, with their plans touching more than $360 million (including money in life insurance policies and assets under management in investments). As a financial professional, he has been broadcast on radio stations 1220 WKRS, 1050 WLIP, 780 WBBM and 720 WGN, and has appeared in Financial Advisor Magazine, the Northwestern University School of Journalism, and Wall Street Select.

Mike frequently teaches financial education classes for a nonprofit speakers' bureau at local colleges.

Through his work with various advisory boards, he has been responsible for training more than 2,000 advisors.

He is also a member of the Institute of Business and Finance (IBF), and the Better Business Bureau (BBB).

Mike also holds many financial seminars for various charities such the American Cancer Society and Alzheimer's Association, as well as many local charities and other nonprofits. On a personal note, Mike and his wife, Leah, have two children: Mikey, fourteen, and Ella, two. Mike enjoys cooking and entertaining with family and friends, boating, traveling, and is an avid Chicago Cubs and Bears fan. He and his family members donate a portion of their time every month, teaching others about Bible truths.

Contact Us

If anything in this book has resonated with you or if you have questions about the ideas contained therein, please, reach out to our office.

MLN Retirement Planning, Inc.
Phone: 844-801-1860 | Fax: 847-510-0990
Email: info@mlnrp.com
Website: https://mlnrp.com

Made in the USA
Monee, IL
28 July 2020